KU-064-663

CONTEMPORARY
TRANSFORMATIONS
OF RELIGION

UNIVERSITY OF
NEWCASTLE UPON TYNE
PUBLICATIONS

CONTEMPORARY TRANSFORMATIONS OF RELIGION

―――

The Riddell Memorial Lectures
Forty-fifth Series
delivered at the
University of Newcastle upon Tyne
on 2, 3, 4 December 1974

BY

BRYAN WILSON

Reader in Sociology
in the University of Oxford
and Fellow of All Souls

OXFORD UNIVERSITY PRESS
LONDON   OXFORD   NEW YORK
1976

Oxford University Press, Ely House, London W. 1

GLASGOW NEW YORK TORONTO MELBOURNE WELLINGTON
CAPE TOWN IBADAN NAIROBI DAR ES SALAAM LUSAKA ADDIS ABABA
DELHI BOMBAY CALCUTTA MADRAS KARACHI DACCA
KUALA LUMPUR SINGAPORE HONG KONG TOKYO

ISBN 0 19 713914 0

© *University of Newcastle upon Tyne 1976*

*All rights reserved. No part of this publication may be reproduced,
stored in a retrieval system, or transmitted, in any form or by any means,
electronic, mechanical, photocopying, recording, or otherwise, without the
prior permission of Oxford University Press*

*Printed in Great Britain
at the University Press, Oxford
by Vivian Ridler
Printer to the University*

For Sylvia and Martin

PREFACE

To be invited to deliver the Riddell Lectures at the University of Newcastle is both an honour and a challenge. I should like to record my gratitude for both, though my readers must judge whether I merited the honour, and whether my performance met the challenge of dealing with a religious subject of general interest to an audience that included not only members of the University, but also many members of the Newcastle general public. To present something of significance in three lectures is an exercise in both selection and compression, and perhaps I made the task no easier by my conviction that in discussing changing religious consciousness, it is necessary to look beyond the established Churches and beyond our own society. Sociological insight is acquired from comparative analysis, and our understanding of the changing nature of religion in the Western world is complemented by an awareness of transformations in religious expression that are occurring in societies at other levels of development.

The context of my discussion is the process of secularization, which I believe can be shown to be a broad, if albeit uneven, evolutionary process. In the first lecture, I try to indicate the evidence for saying that religious commitment and the belief in the power of the supernatural are declining in the modern world. In the second lecture, I devote myself to new religious movements in the West and in the Third World, and contrast their social significance. Whereas new Western movements have usually fostered ideas and practices drawn from traditional and pre-technical cultures, the new movements in the Third World are imported from, or inspired by, Western models. Western sects lead Third World peoples away from the plethora of indigenous magical belief to new, voluntaristic patterns of religious adherence: their votaries learn a new style of personal dedication, social obligation, and even a type of civic commitment. Through these movements, men learn how to do things for themselves, and in that lies, in nascent form, the secularizing thrust of these, as yet profoundly religious, movements. In the third lecture, I take up questions raised by the emergence of new cults in the Western world, and the extent to which they represent either a counterforce to secularization, as some have suggested, or the likely seed-beds of an alternative culture. These cults, oversung as evidence of the persistence of religion by some who should know better but who today have perhaps no other religious song to sing, I regard as having a rather different significance. Their growth, transient appeal, decay, and eventual replacement by other enthusiasms, appear to me to be evidence of the trials of the human spirit in a world in which new techniques and increasingly rational procedures dominate man's social experience. They tell us that living in secular society is painful, and they intimate modern man's permanent condition of bereavement at the loss of community. But they do not provide the basis for a new religious culture.

My response to the challenge of the Riddell Lectures was at every point assisted by the thoughtful arrangements made for me by Miss J. Christie of the University of Newcastle, and by the kindness and hospitality of various members of the University, all of whom I should like to take this opportunity to thank. Several young sociologists at the University of California, by no means all of whom would agree with my interpretation of the contemporary transformations of religion and their significance, generously permitted me to cite or paraphrase information that they had uncovered and which they had presented in conference papers. I should like to thank Gregory Johnson, Jean Messer, Donald Stone, Alan Tobey, and James S. Wolfe. Finally, I should like to express my appreciation to Mrs. Rona Koretz for her inexhaustible patience in typing a much amended manuscript.

All Souls College
Oxford

CONTENTS

I

The Changing Faith and the Changing Churches

PERHAPS the most significant aspect of our conception of what it means to be modern, is the idea that we can consciously change the character of society and the conditions of our lives. Most of our present-day concern—in economics, politics, public affairs, education, and even in entertainment—is concern with change: coping with involuntary change or planning deliberate change. We are committed to the idea that we can *make the future*, by conscious planned activity. It is almost as if change in itself, and for itself, were the cardinal value of our society —the only value that we have got left. In almost all our social institutions we accept the idea of change—from the public area of international economic planning for decades ahead, to the trivialities of everyday consumption for which today we are everywhere exhorted to buy only 'the latest', the things that are *new*. We plan change even in the most intimate areas of our lives: where once we thought that consequences were God's will, we now deliberately programme, regulate, and organize our own future—in family planning.

The one social institution in which change is much less deliberately planned is religion—even in the most formal and organized part of the institution of religion, the Churches, there is much less conscious commitment to change than in other departments of social life, and such planning as does occur is more directed to adjusting to the effects of change in other areas of society than to stimulating innovation for its own sake. Religion, unlike other commodities in our lives, is not pressed upon us—to use the advertising slogan—as something 'New, new, new'. Indeed, the Churches have usually proclaimed themselves as offering not new experience or new wisdom, but old, eternal verities. Religious truth is presented as changeless: in the words of the Gloria 'As it was in the beginning, is now and ever shall be', or as the Psalmist puts it, 'his truth endureth from generation to generation'.

Even when new religious movements have arisen, they have very often done so, not by proclaiming to offer new beliefs and practices, but rather by claiming to restore the pristine faith and order of the past—of the medieval Church, in the case of Tractarian Anglicans of the last century; of the primitive Church, in the case of the Methodists; to the New Testament or the Old, in the case of any one of a dozen movements such as the Plymouth Brethren, the Seventh-Day Adventists, and Jehovah's Witnesses.

Yet it is clear that religion has changed and changed profoundly, and, although in part this has come about as ecclesiastical authorities have tried to cope with the effects on church life of developments occurring in the wider society, by far the most significant changes have come from a popular groundswell as people have made new choices about what to believe, and what to do about what they believe. The process has been spontaneous, as men throughout the world have been deserting their gods, sometimes turning to new ones, or turning to the old ones in new ways.

The diffusion of new religious attitudes is not necessarily less important for society than the conscious process of legislated change in other social institutions. Religion is the repository of custom and the custodian of social values expressed in the most general and elevated form. Religious change is thus cultural change. All cultures have traditionally defined moral behaviour, designated what was worthy and what worthless, prescribed what men might do in their social involvements and—more important— what they might not do. A pattern of constraint is indispensable for orderly social life, and religion has traditionally been a constraining force, particularly in more developed societies. The clergy may not always have known it, and some contemporary clergy, caught up in the fashions of change, may even choose to forget it, but religion has been a primary agency of social control and of socialization. Part of its business has been to discipline the emotions, to circumscribe the occasions on which emotions may be expressed, and to prescribe the forms of its expression— for emotion is the most powerful threat to civilized human life (whether it comes from the passions of football hooligans, joyous at victory or frustrated in defeat, or from the cumulative hatred of Jew-baiting Nazi stormtroopers, or from the lust of inadequately socialized psychopaths). It should not, therefore, be supposed, simply because religious change arises very largely from personal decisions, from changing dispositions, and changing social consciousness, that it is less significant for the quality of social life than the legislation of governments bent on amending, or destroying, particular aspects of social structure.

Religious change is of many kinds—in beliefs, attitudes, behaviour, and institutions. It extends beyond the confines of the Churches, as traditionally organized, and beyond religious practice and belief of a conventional kind, to the new patterns of contemporary religiosity emerging in a variety of new movements. At the same time, I do not share the view that religion is to be seen in every act to which man turns his hand. Unlike some sociologists of religion, I do not regard the Rolling Stones, because of the enthusiasm they engender, as the modern-day equivalents of Moody and Sankey. Nor do I believe that washing the car, even if done religiously every Sunday morning, constitutes a religious act—or that it is an expression of man's 'ultimate concern' in the modern world. I do not accept the idea that the human search for affection, including sexual gratification, is to be seen as modern man's 'invisible religion'.[1] Thus, while regarding religion as something that transcends the traditional Churches, I also regard it as pertaining only to those activities that make some explicit reference to a supernatural source of values.

Contemporary transformations of religion appear to me to be of a kind, an extent, and a rapidity previously unknown in human history, even though there was perhaps never any period in which religion did not change. But whereas past change was often slow, even at times imperceptible or at least unperceived, in the last decade or two we have had the ubiquity of change very forcefully borne in upon us. Until not so very long ago men and societies were oriented to the past. It was the past which established precedents for the present: it was the past from which propriety, wisdom, morality, decency, and the sense of order were thought to come. A knowledge of history was seen as the best liberal education, necessary especially for people entering, for example, public service. In the last few decades, and conspicuously in the last two, that has changed. Our orientation is no longer to the past, but to

[1] For the exposition of this thesis see Thomas Luckmann, *The Invisible Religion*, New York: Macmillan, 1967.

the present and the future. A society that is increasingly preoccupied with conscious and deliberate planning, with long-term investment, with the attempt to construct the social order—once thought to be in some way 'natural' and 'given', perhaps 'God-given'—is now irrevocably committed to the future. Instead of a knowledge of history, a knowledge of the social sciences is now thought to be the appropriate training for those entering public service: instead of looking for past wisdom, for precedent, we look for predictive certainties. Instead of asking what Father did in this or that situation, as men always did in the past eras of human history, we assume that Father's moral wisdom must be as outdated as his technical knowledge surely is.

The Christian faith, like other literate religions, is rooted in a sense of history. The emphasis on the past, on God's past dealings with man, on promises made and kept, on prophecies fulfilled, indicates the ideological commitment to the idea of God's continuing purposes. The truths of the faith were thought to be timeless: they were discovered in the past and believed to have relevance for the present and the future. Religious institutions, too, came to emphasize precedent. They legitimated their provisions and procedures by reference to the past. Their sense of morality was conservative. In deliberating on *what* shall be done— our social policies—and *how* it shall be done—our social organization and techniques—modern society has given up the precedents and lessons of the past, as no longer relevant and, in consequence, the role and place of religion in society has been severely disrupted. The future orientation of modern man has affected both the institutions of faith—the Churches—and the content of the faith of the ordinary man.

B

All the evidence from our own times suggests that, at least in the western world, Christian faith is in serious decline. What is true of the institutions of the Church appears also to be true of the belief and the practice of the majority of men. Religion, particularly in its traditional form, has become socially less and less significant. Most modern men, for most of their time, in most of their activities, are very little touched—if they are touched at all—by any direct religious intimations. Even those who count themselves as believers, who subscribe to the tenets of a Church, and who attend services regularly, nevertheless operate in social space in which their beliefs about the supernatural are rendered in large part irrelevant.

The moral prescriptions of Christianity were relevant for interpersonal relations, for face-to-face contacts, for the intimacies of the family, courtship, friendship, and neighbourliness. But they have much less immediate application to the mass society, with its impersonal and anonymous interaction of role-performers, whose lives impinge on each other in highly automated ways, in which groups and collectivities of men are composed not of those who actually know each other as people, but who are united only because they work in the same mammoth organization, live in the same shapeless conurbation, depend for a livelihood on the export or the import of the same commodities—in short, who share an impersonal interest, or who are prepared to define themselves by the same abstract category, whose sense of themselves is merely that of a 'class'. The moral intimations of Christianity do not belong to a world ordered by conveyor belts, time-and-motion studies, and bureaucratic organization. The very thought processes which these devices demand of men, leave little place for the operation of the divine. The modern world is increasingly a rationally-constructed environment. Its technological basis, its electronic equipment, its computers, its laser beams, its pre-stressed concrete, and its mechanical apparatus dominate and organize an ever greater part of human activity. What place is there in this environment for the intervention of the supernatural? The world is increasingly a rational construct of man's own devising. Religion remains for those other, left over, areas of personal belief and family life, and it seems to me true to say that these are increasingly only the 'recessive' side of human experience.

All this we may contrast with the life of the community of the past. Work was then undertaken with kinsmen and neighbours— well-known persons with whom the individual had life-long relationships and with whom he shared common assumptions about nature and society. The supernatural appeared to enter intimately into work relationships, into the very stuff—the products directly of nature —on which work was undertaken.

It is, of course, one thing to show that social circumstances are propitious (or unpropitious) for belief in the supernatural, and quite another to establish the actual extent of belief. To show that religious truths should have appeared plausible is not to show that they were widely entertained. Those who reject the thesis that a secularization process has been at work in the world over a very long span of time, often object that the very hypothesis of secularization implies that 'once upon a time' there was an age of faith from which modern man has fallen away.[2] They then ask just when was that age of faith, and point to the evidence that the Middle Ages too had their sceptics,

[2] This argument is put forward by David Martin, 'The Secularization Question', *Theology* (February 1973), p. 82.

that the Church authorities even then complained about laxity in religious observance, and that men engaged in a wide range of immoral behaviour, in which they appeared little affected by religious influences. I have no doubt that there never was a Christian age of faith in that sense, an age in which one could say, as Peter Laslett has said,

All our ancestors were literal Christian believers all of the time. . . . Not everyone was equally devout of course, and it would be simple-minded to suppose that none of these villagers ever had their doubts. Much of their devotion must have been formal, and some of it mere conformity. But their world was a Christian world and their religious activity was spontaneous not forced on them from above.[3]

What there was, I think, was not one age, but many ages, in which men were disposed to believe in the supernatural. Without seeking to make any fine distinctions—and they are distinctions notoriously difficult to draw—between magic and religion, it can be said that there was a diffuse, pervasive, at times perhaps internally self-contradictory, willingness to believe in the existence and the operation of forces and beings of a supernatural kind. This is not of course 'an age of faith' as a Christian would choose to think of it, but rather man's long pre-modern history of belief in spirits, gods, demons, spells, and witches. The evidence for such belief is abundant. A great deal of what the Christian of the Middle Ages complained of was of just such magical ideas—scepticism about the Christian faith did not imply no beliefs at all, but often a belief in older nostrums, other aids to salvation and reassurance, more 'present helps in trouble' than those that the Church appeared to provide.

3 Peter Laslett, *The World We Have Lost*, London: Methuen, 1965, pp. 71–2.

Similarly, if we turn to primitive societies: when early travellers declared that the savages were entirely devoid of religion, all that they meant was that they were not Christians. One traveller, Sir Samuel Barker went further. He told the Ethnological Society of London in 1866 that the Dinka and Shilluk of the Upper Nile had no religion 'nor is the darkness of their minds enlightened by even a ray of superstition'.[4] Today anthropologists would reject any such interpretation. Far from having no religion, primitive man very often had religion to the exclusion of almost everything else. We can see from the innumerable devices and symbols of such societies that men were preoccupied with the supernatural, with warding off evil and invoking good by means that, in general, we should now regard as superstitious. We know how often such forces were invoked and how often men were cautioned about the presence of the untoward. The written records and the visible remains of earlier cultures indicate the ubiquity of belief in one sort of supernatural power or another. Contemporary studies of tribal societies, and indeed of traditional cultures, bear testimony to the same all-pervasive religious dispositions—and we may say 'religious' as long as by 'religious' we do not mean Christian or sophisticated, coherent, doctrinally-reinforced ideologies.

In what Christians commonly regard as 'the age of faith'—the age, let us say, of Innocent III—we see a rather different manifestation of religious commitment. We see the apotheosis of Church control over society, not in the uniformity of devotion, but because the imprint of faith and order demanded by ecclesiastical authority dominated the social framework. Life was effectively regulated, at

---

[4] Cited by Godfrey Leinhardt, *Social Anthropology*, London: Oxford University Press, 1964, p. 146.

least in its public concerns, by the demands of the Church. The Church controlled not only the moral fabric of society (perhaps that least of all), but the formal processes of political, juridical, commercial, and social intercourse— the institutional operation of society. In economic affairs, the Church exercised quasi-monopolistic control operating in what we might nowadays describe as 'restraint of trade'. As far as it could, it regulated processes of production, consumption, and distribution, and by regulation, sustained in large measure at law, it sought to restrain the impulses of men. Society was ordered to effect the glorification of God, to protect the Church, to make plain the afterlife of the righteous and the unrighteous, but all that did not, of course, ensure equal and uniform dedication to God in the hearts of men. Even for that age, 'the age of faith' is perhaps a misnomer: we should refer only to the age of religiously-prescribed social order.

The control of the Church over social institutions gave it no final control over the fears, fetishes, and fantasies of men, nor of the means to safeguard men from these things. The Christian faith offered one means of salvation, which, although it claimed exclusive legitimacy, had to compete with others. Men mixed that faith with other prescriptions, pagan, magical, heretical, or superstitious, and sometimes even their Christian practice was underwritten by superstitious beliefs (as in the case of Christian baptism, right up to modern times).[5] Religion had not yet eliminated magic in the European Middle Ages any more than Islam had eliminated local magic in North Africa by the beginning

[5] An interesting example of the reinforcement of religious attitudes by superstition is provided by M. E. James, *Family, Lineage, and Civil Society: a Study of society, politics, and mentality in the Durham Region, 1500–1640*, Oxford: Clarendon Press, 1974.

of the twentieth century. Indeed, the Christian Church itself grappled earnestly, as with a *genuine* enemy, with witchcraft, devil-worship, animism, and even with ancestral cults. Men were the recipients of a many-sided, often muddled inheritance of faiths, and sought their temporal and spiritual salvation by a variety of not always reconcilable means. The age of Christian institutions was not an age of faith, but of faiths, and that perhaps is all that need be asserted to make the point about the process of secularization.

Over a very long period we can observe a gradual, uneven, at times an oscillating, trend, the general direction of which is none the less unmistakable, in the nature of human consciousness, towards what might be called a 'matter-of-fact' orientation to the world. The process of eliminating magical thinking, belief in the possibility of manipulating the empirical world by non-empirical means has a long history extending back into Judaism (against the Baalim). Christianity, like many world religions, had its own ambiguous moments in the face of penetrative magic, and its own regressions in admitting the magical under the pressure of persistent, lingering folk-religions, but the process of elimination reached its apogee in the spirit of Puritanism.[6] When immanentist religion, which magic so fully characterizes, was finally made unrespectable by the insistence on the complete transcendance of the Puritan God, who now dealt only remotely with mankind, the ground was laid for the acquisition, by increasing bodies of men, of a rational empirical orientation to the world.

---

[6] On the eradication of magic, see Max Weber, *The Sociology of Religion* (trans. Ephraim Fischoff) London: Methuen, 1965, and more specifically for Britain, Keith Thomas, *Religion and the Decline of Magic*, London: Weidenfeld and Nicolson, 1971.

Faith, in such an age was itself faith in the remote: God was all but banished from the world that he was credited with creating. Man took the centre of the stage, even though it was still believed that God had written the script that in his life-span man was to act out. But like the author of a play, God was no longer of importance to its performance, and was not responsible for it. Puritanism established a more roundabout relation between man's activity and God's plan for him. It rejected any idea that man could influence God, or that man could at all affect his own salvation.

Both of these emphases were, of course, ways of demanding more intense faith from men. But in the longer run, and for some men the longer run was not so long, it was a way of making God, and faith in Him, irrelevant to life activities. In particular, it was a way of making men conscious of their social being in an entirely new way, independent of spiritual or supernatural forces in the universe. The emergence of industrial man, technological man (I refrain from saying capitalist man simply because the process was not substantially different as between capitalist and socialist societies) was a process of transforming human consciousness, and that process was the equivalent psychological development of the sociological process by which the spirit of capitalism emerged from the Protestant ethic.

The consequence of this slow process of change in the thinking of men has been steadily to make religious belief and practice—and most of all, conventional, traditional religious belief and practice—difficult for modern man. This difficulty does not stem merely from the fact that some of the embellishments of Christian faith, whether relatively recent embellishments such as harvest festivals, or ancient ones such as stained-glass windows, antiphonal masses, priestly vestments, and high altars, have become functionally irrelevant to modern life. Nor does it arise because some of the biblical prescriptions for personal and moral comportment (such as 'above all things, swear not', or the demand that women keep silent in the churches, or wear hats at worship, nor even Paul's exhortation to celibacy) seem either intrinsically trivial or utterly contradictory of the assumptions of our times. The difficulty occurs at a more fundamental level—in the irreconcilability of the suppositions of faith in the supernatural and its arbitrary unexplained authority, and the suppositions that underlie all other activities and operations in which modern men engage in their everyday lives. The sense of contradiction affects not only Christianity, of course. It affects all the ancient creeds in the face of modernity: the dietetic demands on the Jew; the caste obligations of the Hindu; even the exactions of Ramadan on the conscientious Muslim, stand in ever sharper contrast to the needs, functions, and rhythms of the present-day world.

A distinction is to be made between the faith of men and the institutions of religion in society, and once this distinction is made we can see that the so-called 'age of faith' was merely the age of the institutional Church. We have relatively little direct evidence about the incidence of faith from earlier times, but for recent and contemporary transformations of religion we do have evidence both about individual faith and institutional religion. Our evidence about the changing faith of men—that is about their inner feelings, rather than their support for religious institutions —comes primarily from attitude surveys and questionnaires. I happen to be one of those sociologists who had

a persisting wariness about questionnaire surveys long
before their lamentable inaccuracy was revealed by a
recent General Election: and I have remained generally
unimpressed by the casuistry of the opinion pollsters in
their explanations of errors that they have signally failed
to concede. Ask a man about his beliefs and he is certainly
'put on the spot' to answer a question for the pollster that
he may very well never ask himself. The technique is
clinical, and there is not usually any prolonged attempt to
establish real rapport with the respondent. The question
is asked out of context, and outside the normal associations
of the individual's everyday concerns. The replies are
necessarily forced into codes that can be easily tabulated:
paradoxically, they are responses that are neither spontaneous nor considered. Worst of all, those who design
the questionnaires are often lacking in any prolonged or
serious study of the history and philosophy of the subjects
on which they have embarked on a questionnaire survey.
Yet, acknowledging all these limitations, the data of such
surveys are the best data that we have.

As far as we can see, it appears that dramatic transformations have been occurring in matters of religion, even
in relatively short periods of the recent past—and these
changes fit well enough with the plausible speculations
that I offered earlier. Thus, whereas in 1970 some polls
discovered that 88 per cent of people in Britain professed
to believe in God, and 45 per cent thought of God as a
personal being, in the most recent survey only 64 per cent
professed to believe in God—29 per cent saying that God
was a person, and 35 per cent saying that he was some sort
of Spirit or Life Force. The number who believe in life
after death has fallen, too. In 1968 a Gallup Poll showed
that 54 per cent of the people professed to believe in heaven

(although only 23 per cent believed in Hell): in 1974, asked a somewhat different question about the afterlife, only 39 per cent believed that there was life after death, while 35 per cent believed that there was not.[7] All the evidence is towards the decline of belief in the supernatural, and the rejection of the idea that the supernatural has any significant influence in the everyday life of modern man.

Not only are men disposed to give less credence to the supernatural, and particularly in its conventionally received Christian formulations, but they are now—and this is a relatively recent change—strongly convinced that religion has diminishing importance in the social order. For a long time, even when it was apparent that individual belief was waning, and even though church attendances were falling, men appeared to be still impressed by the institution of the Church. They believed that the Church, and through it, religion, still exerted considerable influence in society. That moment has passed. Today, fewer than 10 per cent believe that the influence of religion is increasing, while 70 per cent think it decreases. Not only do fewer people believe, but everyone now knows that fewer believe, and this very knowledge diminishes the credit of the Church. Despite impressive buildings, an established place in public life, and the dignity accorded to Church leaders, it becomes clear to all that the Church is losing its social significance. In everyday life there is perhaps less respect for the cloth than there was, and certainly the mass media find it hard to present clergymen without suggesting, however faintly, that their presumed acquaintance with the things of the next world is best conveyed by

[7] Figures for 1974 are from Louis Harris International Speedsearch, *Spiritual Attitudes Survey*, 1974.

suggesting that they have a very tenuous understanding of this one.

The presidency that the Church once exercised over social life has gone, as other agencies have assumed the functions that it once fulfilled. Instead of being the local centre of community life, the Church has become more narrowly and specifically a religious centre, segregated and encapsulated. Whereas once the clergyman, if he was a diligent incumbent, was also the educator, the guardian of community morals, the social worker, at times even the magistrate, the sick visitor (when not actually a medical adviser), today, these roles have been taken over by others. The political influence of the clergy, which sometimes amounted to actual power, has also gone. As the principal agent for communication of information from the State, the priest once had, if not a monopoly, then a privileged role, as a communicator of values, opinions, and dictates, in the age before the development of literacy: but this function is no longer his.

In its steadily more confined sphere, the institution lived on, occupying premises and often enjoying the appearance of a greater and more significant presence in the life of nations than was warranted by the distribution of religious dispositions in the population. Paradoxically, ordinary people were in the main contented with this arrangement. Although not religious themselves, they did not mind the gentle influence of religion in the life of the nation. They might even send their children to Sunday school, not solely for the custodial function that it provided on Sunday afternoons but because in some sense there was a recognition of the desirability of a stable moral order and a continuing traditional culture. And in any case, what other agency was there to fulfil the function of moral socializa-

Compare religion with other
institutions in the 1970's
-re just

The Changing Faith and the Changing Churches 17

Symptom
of British
Tumour
Delini

tion and social control, and to give suitably solemn expression to elevated values? Thus the institution had for some time a tacit measure of support from men whose religious opinions were neutral or even negative. The Church—or the churches—still looked solid and reliable. They had a presence, their personnel had a dignity, derived no doubt from the solemnity and seriousness of their concerns, which, even for the faithless was not without value as a reassurance of social order and civic decency. And all this, I suspect, was behind the opinion poll surveys in the 1950s and early 1960s when the majority continued to say that they believed that the influence of religion was increasing. By the 1970s that comforting illusion had gone.

The public's new conviction that the influence of religion is declining has not come from close analysis of facts and figures. It is merely a general impression that somewhat belatedly has been borne in upon people. The effect of waning authority is nowhere more clearly evident than in the Church's loss of moral influence, which has been followed by its loss of moral certainty. Thus it is that, although the Church still preaches against sin, just what churchmen now consider to be sin has in some respects changed. This can be seen very clearly in the changing attitudes to birth control in the Church of England. In 1908 the Lambeth Conference declared that it regarded with alarm

the growing practice of the artificial restriction of the family, and earnestly calls upon all Christian people to discountenance the use of all artificial means of restriction as demoralizing to character and hostile to national welfare.[8]

In 1916 a memorandum from the Committee of Anglican

[8] Report of the Lambeth Conference of 1908.

Bishops was more emphatic, giving 'an unhesitating judgment' that the use of artificial appliances and drugs was 'at once dangerous, demoralizing and sinful' and was

condemned as unnatural by healthy instinct. . . . A society in which it is practised will lose all delicacy of feeling and refinement . . . which comes of keeping the natural instincts of modesty and reserve untarnished.[9]

By 1958 the Church had changed its idea of what was sinful, and even pronounced family planning to represent

an extension of the responsible use of science into the realm of procreation in the immediate interest of the family and the more remote but no less real interest of society at large.[10]

Even where the official attitude to sin has remained nominally unchanged, as, for example, in the case of homosexuality, the Church no longer seeks to have its conception of sin underwritten by the State which in the past accepted that what religiously was 'sin', socially was 'crime'. And where the Church has continued to try to influence the modern state on moral matters, its advice has often been rejected: a case in point was the recent campaign of the Church in Italy for the rescindment of the divorce law (even though that law, even then, gave people the opportunity to seek divorce only in very narrowly circumscribed cases).

Ideas about sin have changed in the Church not because churchmen have been in the van of social change, but because they have belatedly acknowledged changes that have already occurred, and have caught a glimpse of them-

[9] Evidence given to the Commission on the Declining Birthrate, 1916: Memorandum submitted by the Committee of Anglican Bishops.

[10] *The Family in Contemporary Society*, The Report of a Group convened at the request of the Archbishop of Canterbury, London: SPCK, 1958.

selves frozen in what, for modern man, seemed to be absurd postures. Since the idea of sin is somewhat attenuated, so the old religious sanctions have also been largely forsaken, and it is even difficult for modern man to imagine that the fear of hellfire was used as a deterrent of various sorts of social conduct in the not so distant past. The 'decline of hell' has been a relatively long process, symptomatic perhaps of a basic shift in society—a shift from society conceived as a moral order to society conceived primarily as a technical order.[11]

As the crude force of threats of hell and blandishments of heaven were slowly abandoned in the churches from the Reformation onwards, so greater dependence was placed on the internalization by individuals of approved moral constraint; encouragement was given to the cultivation of conscience. The balance shifted from social control to socialization, from the use of promises of fear and reward increasingly to the development of a sense of guilt and of moral integrity. In British history, in particular, this development of self-control, the diffusion throughout society of conscientious concern and disinterested goodwill, was perhaps the apogee of social morality. But times have changed again. From an age in which it was enlightened to suggest that people should be taught to control themselves (rather than to be controlled by external agents) we have now come to a time when a permissive society tells us that even self-control is bad; that there is something worse than misbehaviour, namely, that individuals should be thwarted in doing what they want. Thus we have gone from the external attempt to impose moral control largely by religious threats, through an age in

[11] See D. P. Walker, *The Decline of Hell*, London: Routledge, 1964, and D. G. Rowell, *Hell and the Victorians*, Oxford: Oxford University Press, 1974.

which what was sought was internal control, attained by the religiously directed cultivation of conscience, to modern times in which any sort of control, external or internal, has ceased to be a religious or moral matter, an age in which, indeed, some contemporary politically-minded psychiatrists have suggested that control itself, whether social control or self-control, is almost immoral.

Of course, modern society, permissive as it is, does not lack modes of control. We have our traffic lights, our radar traps, our parking meters; we have the conveyor belt, the time-clock, the time-and-motion study, the planning authority, the insurance system, the identikit, the credit agency, and the Trades Description Act. All these items illustrate the extent to which control has become a matter for mechanical and bureaucratic devices. It has become impersonal and amoral, a matter for routine techniques and unknown officials. Our world has been *de*-moralized as we have replaced human involvement in many areas of activity by technical controls, and as we have reduced human concern in other areas by the new ethos of permissiveness—the ethos of 'who cares?'. As our society has become less dependent on moral regulation, and as our relations to each other have become more role-regulated and less personally involved, so the functions of religion have declined, and men feel less need for religion.

The decline of faith, and of the influence of faith, has not left the institutional structure of the Churches unchanged. Tacitly, modern society simply denies the authority of the Churches, by ignoring them. And that denial affects the confidence of churchmen in their own claims to authority. Today, if an archbishop expresses concern about some social problem, such as the influence of television, or the effects on family life when large numbers of women go out to work, he is less likely to pronounce policy on the strength of Holy Writ, or church doctrine, than to call for the establishment of an investigating committee of experts. And those experts are more likely to be social scientists than churchmen or theologians. When modern man seeks answers to social problems, whether he does so through a Royal Commission or through a B.B.C. panel, clerics are a class of people who are now among the least likely people to be asked.

If this is the current condition of faith, can we be surprised that the traditional institutions of religion increasingly lack public support? Some churchmen realized that church attendances were falling behind population growth from at least the second half of the nineteenth century. Only the Roman Catholics, whose growth was attributable both to immigration and, in later periods, to differential fertility, had reason for confidence, but, as a minority Church often identified with alien countries, the Roman Church in Britain appears to have kept itself from the public view.

If there were already faint indications of religious decline before the First World War, the evidence became inescapable after the Second, and this not only in Britain, but also in Europe. In England the Easter Day communicants of the Church of England fell from just under 10 per cent of the population aged over fifteen years in the period just before the Great War, to 6·5 per cent in 1960, and 5·6 per cent in 1968. Whereas in 1930 the electoral roll of the Church of England had nearly 3,700,000 people inscribed, in 1968 there were fewer than 2,700,000 from a much larger eligible population. Even in the much shorter run some changes have been dramatic: thus, whereas in 1956 more than 60 per cent of all live births in

C

England had been baptized in the Church of England, in
1968 the proportion was less than 50 per cent. Nor had the
Nonconformists done any better. The Baptists in the
British Isles had fallen from 418,000 members in 1911
and 335,000 in 1951, down to 263,000 in 1971. In the period
from 1959 to 1971, the Methodist membership in Great
Britain had shrunk from 733,000 to 600,000. The Con-
gregationalists in England and Wales who had had 440,000
in 1935 had lost more than half that number by 1965, and
by 1973 were fewer than 200,000, a decline that continued
despite their union with the Presbyterian Church of
England.[12]

By the late 1960s only about 3.5 per cent of the population of England attended the Church of England on an
ordinary Sunday. Between 10 and 12 per cent of the population of England and Wales attend a church on Sundays,
but this figure is so high only because for Roman Catholics
attendance is an obligation, but even among Catholics
decline has occurred. Between 1966 and 1969 according
to parish priest returns, Catholic attendance at mass in
England and Wales fell by almost 6 per cent—although
the Catholic population fell hardly at all.[13] The decline in
church attendance among Catholics on the Continent was
already evident in the 1950s and early 1960s. Surveys in
forty-seven towns in Germany showed that there had been
a general fall of about 5 or 6 per cent in attendance at mass
between 1956 and 1963. In the course of two decades mass

[12] These figures are from *The Church of England Yearbook*; *Minutes of the
Methodist Conference*; *Congregational Yearbook*; *Baptist Handbook*: various
dates.

[13] This estimate is put forward by Robert Currie and Alan Gilbert in an as
yet unpublished manuscript, 'A Statistical Survey of Church Membership in
Britain and Ireland since 1700' (available as a Report to the Social Science
Research Council, London).

attendance had by 1966 fallen by over 13 per cent in Amsterdam and Rotterdam, and figures for those cities, with 39 and 33 per cent of the Catholic population still attending at mass, were high when compared to figures for some Belgian and French cities—22 per cent in Liège, 20 per cent in Bordeaux, and 26 per cent in Nancy.[14]

Attendance figures are easily misinterpreted. One must remember that the very act of going to church has different meanings in different cultures and in different Christian denominations. In England, with an established Church, many more people claim to belong to the Church of England than actually attend at all regularly: they have what might be called a 'post office' conception of the Church, a service facility that is well distributed over the land area of the country to be available when needed. In the United States, to take a different example, religious adherence is a much more emphatically voluntary act and this may, paradoxically, make attendance a culturally more significant affirmation. Churches there appear often to have community functions that they lack in Europe (perhaps because they cater for a much more mobile population for whom a community centre is otherwise lacking) and this too may be a factor which induces a higher attendance rate in American churches.[15] But even in America the churches have experienced a decline from the late 1950s when a normal Sunday would see over 50 per cent of the population in church: in 1972 only 40 per cent were estimated to be in church on an ordinary Sunday.

[14] The Continental evidence is taken from S. S. Acquaviva, *L'Eclissi del Sacro nella Civiltà industriale*, Milan, Edizioni di Comunità, 3rd edn., 1971, pp. 94, 99, 129.

[15] For a fuller exposition see Bryan Wilson, *Religion in Secular Society*, London: Penguin, 1969.

Attendances among Catholics diminished from 71 to 57 per cent between 1964 and 1972.[16]

The prevalence of the post office conception of the Church might lead one to expect that although many people did not normally attend, none the less, they used the Church when they needed it. Up to a point, this has been the case in the past, but there are signs that even this recourse to the Church is now declining. One indicator must here suffice to support this contention: the use of the churches for marriage ceremonies. Even the relatively unreligious often preferred to have their marriage in a church —the very sense of authentic tradition was appealing. Even that now appears to have a diminished attraction. Thus of marriages solemnized in England and Wales, there has been a declining proportion solemnized in the churches.[17]

Year	Church of England and Church in Wales %	Other churches %	Civil Registry %
1859	81·2	12·3	6·5
1899	67·8	17·2	15·0
1929	56·2	18·1	25·7
1957	49·6	22·4	28·0
1973	36·5	17·9	46·6

Attendance, and recourse to the churches for special functions, are not the only items important to the maintenance of the churches. There has been a relative decline in mission-giving, a decline in the number of churches in use, and a steady relative decline in the stipends of the

[16] Gallup Poll, January 1972.

[17] *Facts and Figures About the Church of England*, London: Church Information Office, 1962, and 1965 (No. 3); and Office of Population Censuses and Surveys, 1974.

clergy of all denominations. In some places there has even
been the sale of treasures—treasures accumulated in much
less affluent days—to finance the contemporary operations
of the church in the age of affluence. Religious economics
is a neglected field, but it can readily be stated that the
proportion of the Gross National Product devoted to the
supernatural has diminished in the course of the centuries.
If one took this argument further and compared tribal
societies with advanced societies, the disproportion would
be even greater. It is a plausible hypothesis that the more
developed the economic techniques of a society, and the
more affluent its circumstances, the lower the proportion
of its productive wealth will be devoted to the supernatural. If that hypothesis is not disconfirmed, it might be
taken as our best indicator of secularization, showing what
man chooses to do with his resources, his energies, and,
by implication, his time.

   The Churches change not only because of their declining
capacity to summon the loyalties and the donations of the
laity. To continue in their traditional functions, they
require the service of a disciplined corps of clergy. Until
relatively recently most European countries have been
self-sufficient in this respect, and have had priests to export
to assist in countries that have never had an adequate
supply. Shortage has always been the case in many Latin
American countries, which have depended on the migration of priests from Spain, Portugal, and Italy. Today,
there is a decline in vocations throughout Europe. Thus,
in the Federal Republic of Germany, the number of intend-
ing Roman Catholic priests admitted to the first year of
seminary training diminished from 544 in 1967 to 314 in
1972. Of those admitted, a falling percentage now achieve
ordination: those ordained in 1966 constituted 58 per cent

of the group admitted to the seminary; in 1972 the proportion had fallen to 24 per cent. Thus, not only do fewer
seek to enter the seminary, but of those few who enter a
much smaller proportion actually emerge as priests. In
Belgium, in 1966, there were 137 ordinations to the secular
priesthood; by 1972, following a steady annual fall, the
number was only 70. In Holland, whereas in 1965 there
were 4,170 secular priests in the Roman Church, in 1972
there were 500 fewer: and since 1968 more priests have
been leaving the priesthood each year than have been
ordained. The picture is even worse in Spain: there were
8,300 vocations for the diocesan clergy in 1961–2; in 1972–3
there were only 2,790—a decrease of more than 60 per
cent. Even in Ireland, admissions to all branches of the
Catholic Church have fallen: the numbers in the diocesan
seminary fell from 254 in 1966 to 184 in 1972; the admis-
sion of priests and lay brothers in religious congregations
fell from 390 in 1966 to 246 in 1972. Among Irish congregations of sisters, a larger number left in 1971 and 1972 than
were admitted.

If one turns to the Roman Catholic religious orders
throughout the world, the story is essentially the same:
between 1967 and 1972 the number of Jesuits in the world
declined by 11·7 per cent; of Franciscans by 14·3 per cent;
of Marist Brothers and Dominicans, each by 16·7 per
cent; of Christian Brothers by 18·3 per cent, and of the
Oblates by over 23 per cent.[18] Despite much jubilation in
1974 about an increase of ordinands in the Anglican Church
in England vocations had, until 1974, been falling steadily.
In the early 1960s over 700 ordinands was normal: in
1974, 346 was cause for rejoicing. At the end of 1969 there

[18] Figures from 'New Forms of Ministries in Christian Communities', *Pro
Mundi Vita*, 50 (1974), pp. 84–6, 89.

were 15,494 active Anglican clergy—less than five years later there were only 13,105. The story for the Non-conformist denominations is essentially the same.[19]

Absolute numbers tell only part of the story, however. If a profession is declining, it is likely also to be suffering from an ageing profile. Unduly high proportions of the aged within a profession are likely to induce slackening morale, to reduce efficiency, to make difficult the continuity of function and—and this is more important for the clerical profession than for any other—to disrupt the transmission of values and traditions. If the normal span of a priest's working life is from 25 years of age to 65 years, in a healthy profession considerably more than half should be under 45. Among the active Anglican clergy, however, in 1969, only 40 per cent were under 45, over 28 per cent were between 55 years and 65 years, and more than 9 per cent were over 65 years of age.[20] The distribution of age among the active Roman Catholic clergy in England was not very different: in 1972 about 40 per cent were under 45 years of age; 43 per cent were between 45 and 65; and over 15 per cent were over 65.[21]

Statistics reveal social processes, but they do not expose the causes of contemporary change, nor do they intimate the type of tensions that currently exist within the Churches. The decline in vocations is obviously related to the reinterpretation of the role of the priest, and to new ideas about liturgy; but it is also related to new conceptions of salvation. The specific incidence of change has varied from one country to another, and the most dramatic change has tended to occur in those denominations or those countries

---

[19] *Church of England Yearbook*, various dates.
[20] Ibid.
[21] 'New Forms of Ministries in Christian Communities', op. cit.

in which there had previously been only a slight relaxation of earlier positions. Thus, among Protestant denominations, it is the large very fundamentalist Lutheran Missouri Synod in the United States which is currently rent by schism, especially among its theologians. In the Catholic Church it was in Holland—for a long time the country which gave the Vatican least trouble, and in the 1940s and 1950s increasingly a source of conscientious missionaries—that serious disruption began in the mid 1960s.[22] And it was in Italy, the heart-land of Catholicism, that some of the more revolutionary positions were widely canvassed in the emergence of a significant underground Church in the late 1960s.[23] The processes of change in the Roman Catholic Church were influenced by the emergence of a militant youth culture and by the serious disruption in the universities that occurred throughout the western world at that time, and which left perhaps indelible scars on the universities in Holland and Italy. Here I can do no more than indicate the main thrust of agitation—for churches without priests, or for the complete laicization of the Church; for communion without sanctified emblems; for changes in the Church's attitude to birth control; and, especially in Italy, for active social involvement of the Church in political affairs, in alliance with the Marxists. Perhaps the most important issue of all has been the demand that priests should be allowed to marry. The Church's rejection of this reform has led many priests,

[22] A detailed analysis is provided in James A. Coleman, *The Evolution of Dutch Catholicism*, Berkeley and Los Angeles: University of California Press, forthcoming.

[23] An analysis of the Italian situation is provided by Gustavo Guizzardi, 'New Religious Phenomena in Italy: Towards a Post-Catholic Era?', VIIIth World Congress of Sociology, Research Committee for the Sociology of Religion, Toronto, 1974.

especially in Holland, to leave the priesthood and some to leave the Church.

Despite the changes within the Catholic Church that followed the Second Vatican Council, the revolutionary movement that began among some priests and young people went further than the bishops ever envisaged, and threatened a significant development of extra-ecclesial religion. The specific foci of revolutionary concern were perhaps of less intrinsic significance than appeared at the time. What many of those involved were discovering, often painfully, was that they could in fact challenge the Church, could threaten the Church, and eventually could live without the Church. For some, this reinterpretation of their position ultimately led to agnostic or political conclusions. Having been in the Church for so long, some priests found that they had to express even their incipient anti-religious dispositions in terms relevant to the religious organization to which they belonged. Only after some years has it become apparent to many of them that their specific struggles for 'change within' were in fact merely the symptomatic sickening for their eventual decision to get out.

Given the changes in the relation of the Church to society, and the role of institutionalized religion in society, it should not be surprising that such profound shuddering should first be felt within the Church by some of those supposedly most deeply committed to it. History reveals similar processes before, particularly in the development of new intellectual perspectives at a time when the Church had a virtual monopoly of intellect—in the Renaissance and again in the nineteenth century. But the challenge to the faith has not taken everyone in the same way. There are many who have been profoundly shocked and disenchanted by the liberal efforts of priests. In Holland there are powerful ultra-conservative and moderate conservative groups which seek to retain the style, the authority, and the formularies of their Church and the more extreme among them have finally and regretfully come to abjure the Pope whom they see as having ceased to be properly Catholic.[24]

In the Catholic Church the crisis of faith has been in large part expressed in quasi-political terms, as in Holland, with the emergence of well-organized pressure groups, each with different demands. In Protestantism change has appeared less dramatic because Church structures were less hierarchic and less rigid, and acceptance of policies of change have had more explicit official approval—not least in the late 1950s and 1960s in a decade of what might be called ecumenical hope. The Churches recognized that, faced with the growing secularity of western society, their own differences were of less consequence than they had formerly supposed—just as, at an earlier stage, they had discovered a similar thing in the mission field. For a time there was hope that, even if the world could not be con- verted, *other* Christians could be brought into the truth. The terms of ecumenism were not always well thought out, and early hopes ran into the sand of difficulties be- tween, and divisions within, the Churches. The laity were often in favour of union as a slogan which they had heard from the clergy, but they were not always prepared for the abandonment of aspects of liturgy and doctrine which union might entail.[25] The clergy, always heavily over-

[24] P. G. McCaffery, 'A Sociological Analysis of the concerns of pressure- groups in the Roman Catholic Church in the Netherlands and in England', *Acts of the 12th Conference on the Sociology of Religion*, Lille: CISR Secretariat, 1973, pp. 239–56.

[25] See David Clark, *Survey of Anglicans and Methodists in Four Towns*, London: Epworth Press, 1965.

represented in ecumenical conversations, often established theoretical and doctrinal agreements, but these were sometimes achieved with a certain deviousness and even a deliberate obscuration of difficulties (as in the Anglican–Methodist formula). But they were less successful in working out the details of organizational amalgamation. It is not without sociological interest that the least centrally organized denominations have proved themselves to be the best able to achieve union—in the United Church of Christ in America, and in the United Reformed Church in Britain.

Ecumenical hope has faded somewhat with the breakdown of the Anglican–Methodist attempt, and the lack of progress among the denominations engaged in the Consultation on Church Union in America. The myth that it was the divisions of the Churches that hindered evangelism has been dispelled. The belief that ecumenism would lead to a more vigorous, growing Church—itself lacking any confirmation in history—has largely evaporated.[26] In a period when the young in particular have assaulted existing structures as alienating and inhuman, the idea of the emergence of ever larger monolithic religious institutions has become less attractive, perhaps particularly to the younger clergy. Uncertainty has increased as vocations have diminished and as Church structures and establishments have run down, to a point where it is clear that contemporary Church problems transcend ecumenical solutions. Divisions have become more evident, in some denominations, particularly as growth has occurred in the more conservative congregations as the more numerous liberal congregations in the same denomination have

[26] For a historical refutation see Robert Currie, *Methodism Divided*, London: Faber, 1968.

declined.[27] Widely divergent beliefs about quite central issues in Christianity exist side by side within the same denomination and, were denominations to declare their positions publicly, these differences might become the occasion for division and even schism.[28] Nor has the new social activism of some of the clergy, conspicuously among the 'campus ministry' in the United States, in the Dominican order, and at the World Council of Churches, in which political postures have often replaced prayerful postures, always appealed to the laity.[29] It is by no means clear that their older clientele will always follow the younger clergy into political campaigns which the laity do not necessarily accept as part of the charter of Christian churchmanship.

Paradoxically the most vigorous grass-roots ecumenical movement of recent years is also potentially the most divisive. The rapid growth of the charismatic movement has brought together Christians of very diverse denominations, from Catholics to Baptists, but it has also created strong differences within individual churches and congregations. The charismatic movement is the one new, widespread, and spontaneous response of Christians both to the crisis of faith and to the crisis of contemporary society. It is based on the belief that the nine gifts of the Spirit, described by Paul in 1 Corinthians 12, are still in operation, and that the faithful may today, as in New Testament times, exercise these gifts—of the word of wisdom, the word of knowledge, faith, healing, miracles, prophecy, discernment

[27] See Dean M. Kelley, *Why Conservative Churches Are Growing*, New York: Harper and Row, 1972.

[28] See Charles Y. Glock and Rodney Stark, *Religion and Society in Tension*, Chicago: Rand McNally, 1965, pp. 86-112.

[29] See P. E. Hammond and R. E. Mitchell, 'Segregation of Radicalism: the Case of the Protestant Campus Ministry', *American Journal of Sociology*, 71, 2 (September, 1965), pp. 133-43.

of spirits, speaking in tongues, and the interpretation of tongues. Among these nine gifts, it is the gift of tongues—glossolalia—that arouses most interest, both among contemporary charismatics and among those opposed to them. In general, the orthodox denominations of Christendom have denied that the gifts of the Spirit remained in operation after New Testament times and have regarded the recorded cases of glossolalia as misplaced enthusiasm occurring in the excitement of religious revivals when not associated with outright heresy. In the nineteenth century the Mormons and the Irvingite Catholic Apostolic Church both gave particular attention to this gift of the Spirit, although only in the Irvingite Church were the gifts accorded institutionalized significance.

At the very beginning of the twentieth century, the modern Pentecostal movement began in the United States, spreading to Scandinavia and to Britain within the course of six or seven years. From that impetus a number of sectarian movements developed, and those within the churches who endorsed the pentecostal phenomena found a current of opposition to their practice within their own denominations. Thus, separated Pentecostal sects arose, which made the exercise of the Spirit gifts, and particularly speaking in other tongues, their very *raison d'être*, since in other respects many of them did not significantly differ in doctrine from a wider body of Christian fundamentalists.[30]

It would not be untrue to say that Christians in the major Churches tended, until very recently, to regard Pentecostalists with considerable contempt—they were enthusiasts, Holy Rollers, spiritual anarchists in 'do it yourself' churches in which the less-educated and lower-class were

[30] On the history of early Pentecostalism see W. J. Hollenweger, *The Pentecostals*, London: SCM Press, 1972.

misled about the nature of the Christian life. Theologians were dismissive about the Pentecostal claim—namely that God required worship in all tongues, whether extant or defunct, and that it was not for man to dispute God's will in this matter. The orthodox had regarded the gifts of the Spirit as a description of a variety of natural abilities which God had distributed among men, or as purported miraculous competences confined to the apostolic age. The lack of cultivated style and of an educated leadership, and the, often exaggerated, stories of the excessive emotionalism that prevailed in Pentecostal meetings, was enough to bring them into ill-repute with other Christians and with the general public. Pentecostal claims of miracles, healings, and prophecies, which were always difficult to substantiate, were discounted. Tongues was the one gift that was widely manifested, and the opinion of orthodox Christians was that what was uttered were not words in any known language, but gibberish, itself the result of infectious emotionalism, or of shamming, or—so some fundamentalists believed— a counterfeit work of the Devil himself.

Until the late 1950s, the Pentecostalists and the phenomena associated with their form of worship remained a manifestation of pariah-Christianity. Then, in 1958, in a wealthy and respectable congregation of the American Episcopal Church, some individuals, led by their priest, began to speak in tongues. The incident which occurred in Van Nuys, California, was reported, and the experience was repeated. Several ordained priests soon became convinced of the authenticity of the Pentecostal experience. Within months, speaking in tongues had become a widely experienced faculty in various churches in the United States. Particularly in prayer meetings, those enthusiastic about the new style of worship met together and encouraged the exercise of the Spirit gifts. New journals devoted to the exposition of the newly accepted explanation of the charismatic experience appeared; after a little while special bookshops were opened, foundations set up, and conferences were instituted to propagate the movement that became known as charismatic renewal. The interdenominational Christian Businessmen's Fellowship International became a particularly important agency in the spread of the new style of religious experience, and within a few years the movement had spread throughout the English-speaking world. In Britain it has been claimed that more than 300 members of the clergy have undergone the charismatic experience, and in the United States there is now an annual conference at Notre-Dame University which draws together several thousand Catholics, among them a considerable number of priests and nuns, both for discussion of and participation in the newly rehabilitated patterns of religious experience. Some estimates suggest that in the United States as many as 300,000 Roman Catholics have become involved in the new movement, and that there are over 700 Episcopal priests, 500 Presbyterian ministers, and 800 Baptist ministers who speak in unknown tongues.[31]

The ecumenical element of charismatic renewal is evident in the way in which the movement has grown up largely in interdenominational prayer meetings. Those participating are understandably disposed to regard their shared experience as a significant, and perhaps

[31] The growth of the Charismatic Renewal Movement is documented by Richard Quebedeaux, 'Charismatic Renewal: The Origins, Development, and Significance of Neo-Pentecostalism as a Religious Movement in the United States and Great Britain, 1901–1973', unpublished D.Phil. thesis, University of Oxford, 1975.

fundamental, bond of fellowship. Even though they have
not deserted their Churches, and certainly have not followed the pattern of the sectarian Pentecostalism of the first
half of the twentieth century, they have undoubtedly come
to place their pentecostal involvement in the forefront of
their Christian lives, whatever the formal creeds of the
churches in which they normally worship. Some congregations have gone over completely to the charismatic cause,
and their members engage together in the exercise of the
gifts, particularly the gift of tongues. So far, the Church
authorities have said little about the new development.
The movement has its opponents in the Churches, but
there has been no authoritative official condemnation, even
though the new Pentecostalism is a very considerable
departure from established patterns of faith and order.
Perhaps the very fact that the Charismatics are the most
vigorous new development in the life of waning Churches
deters those who lack sympathy for the movement from
speaking against it. Perhaps, too, theological certainty is
not what once it was.

Nor have most of the older 'classical' sectarian Pentecostal groups welcomed the more middle-class 'Johnny-
come-lately' exponents of the practice which they have
cherished for half a century or more. The new charismatic
people are not only better educated, but they appear to
share few of the social attitudes, moral prescriptions, and
fundamentalist doctrines accepted by the older Pentecostals. They may distrust the new discovery by middle-
class people of authenticity in the subjective, spontaneous,
and instantaneous, and in particular they may disapprove
of the fact that the new prayer groups do not fit the Spirit-
gifts into an integrated and coherent body of doctrines or
into the institutional life of their churches.

Spontaneity and subjectivism have become powerful elements in contemporary culture. Inner feeling has been widely hailed as more *authentic* than intellectual knowledge. Emotion and the devices to express it and stimulate it which often stem from lower-class groups, under-privileged minorities, such as the Negroes in the United States—from whom Pentecostalism inherited much of its musical and expressive style—are in general favour in the youth culture, in student sub-cultures, in the entertainment culture of our times. It should not surprise us if, against the general background of secularization, the one 'growth sector' within the Churches and within institutionalized religion should mobilize the same dispositions and offer the same rewards. It would be surprising were it otherwise.

D

New Missions to Old Believers

THE traditional Churches are in decline in the western world, and the conventional faith of most ordinary citizens will never again be of the kind that existed, shall we say, before the Great War. Yet, as is evident in the charismatic renewal movement, the contemporary transformations of religion are by no means all of a kind. The most powerful trend is secularization, which occurs as our social organization becomes increasingly dominated by technical procedures and rational planning. But modern society is highly complex, and men are very diversely affected by changes in the social system, and hence are influenced by secularization in varying degrees. The married man with children—buying a home, running a car, working in a factory or an office, carrying insurances, mortgages, hire-purchase obligations, paying income tax and local rates, receiving children's allowances, paying trade-union dues, and maintaining some interest in local conditions, at least as they affect his living standards—is, willy-nilly, heavily involved in, and affected by, the social system. The student, with few long-term obligations, rather ill-defined work-tasks, and variable and personally chosen working hours, with no dependants, no taxes, no insurances, no mortgage payments, and perhaps no car, is very much less affected by the procedures and routines of the social order. These two classes of people are likely to be vulnerable in very different degrees to the secularizing and rationalizing effects of modern society, and to have very different measures of opportunity to escape them. If there are counter-secular trends occurring in society, they are likely to arise among those least heavily involved in the day-to-day routines of the social order.

Secularization is associated with the structural differentiation of the social system—separation of different areas of social activity into more specialized forms. This process occurs with the development of techniques and the extension of the division of labour. Instead of work activity, family life, education, religious practice, the operation of law and custom, and recreation, all being part of each other, and affecting everyone in more or less self-sufficient close-knit small communities, as occurred in large measure in all pre-modern societies, we have highly specialized places, times, resources, and personnel involved in each of these areas of social life, and their efficiency and viability has depended on this process of specialization. For evident reasons, specialization has, particularly in recent centuries, occurred less in that social institution that we designate 'religion' than in any other, and this is one important contribution to the decline of the Churches. Religion has come to be associated much more as one among a number of leisure activities, it exists in that area of free choice of the use of time, energy, and wealth in which the end products of the economy are marketed for consumers. But even among leisure activities, religion is much less organized and, as far as the *effective* use of resources goes, much less capitalized (in the sense that it has much less *working* capital) than is the modern entertainment industry. Religion, after all, depends less on elaborate technical equipment or technically specialized premises, it has a much less calculated rational division of labour among its personnel, and, in consequence, by modern standards—perhaps inappropriate standards in this case, but standards that we have got used to in almost all other spheres of public activity—it is characterized by inefficiency.

The analogy is, of course, slightly inept: we do not think of religion in terms of efficiency or productivity per unit of man-hour cost and investment opportunity; we do not regard priests or Sisters of Mercy as labour-units. But the very fact that these concepts are inept makes the point clear: institutionalized religion operates in a world the language of which, and the assumptions of which, have largely changed. And this is even true in the sphere of leisure activities, into association with which religion has now inadvertently slipped. Even here, its worth is steadily devalued. Our political agencies regard leisure as important in some respects: as the Romans in hard times relied on their circuses, so the modern state channels money into leisure facilities. The State has even created a Ministry of Sport. On the other hand, despite the fact that we have a Church by law established, the whole tendency of the State, for at least 200 years, has been to divest itself of religious commitments and embroilments. Far from anyone thinking that we need a government ministry for religion, the Church of England tussles internally with the pros and cons of severing the State connection altogether or almost altogether. Some churchmen would like the Church to have the power to appoint its own bishops, even if it entailed the loss of episcopal seats in the House of Lords, and just possibly the risk that the Coronation ceremony ceased to be an Anglican monopoly.

The loss by religion of many of its old functions, and

particularly those of social control, and its steady detach-
ment from the main spheres of public life have opened the
way for new patterns of religious practice, divested of all
the ancient associations, and completely unconnected with
the State, the Establishment, or the social system in which
today the lives of most of us are so completely implicated.
Nor has this development been confined to Britain:
indeed, throughout the world there is a phenomenal
growth of new religious movements that are unassociated
with the existing social order, and which very often promise
their votaries something very much better. Not all of these
new movements are themselves world-wide, and they differ
very significantly in style, provenance, and orientation.
They have differential appeal in different cultures, and
movements, some of them of western origin, that are not
succeeding, or not succeeding very well, in Britain may
be flourishing at an unprecedented rate of growth in the
Philippines or in Chile. The defecting groups from, say,
the Roman Catholic Church in Africa, are differently
prompted from those in Holland, although defection
occurs in both places. The movements that have had such
a dramatic impact in Japan are very little known outside
that country, except among Japanese who have emigrated
overseas. Yet, in spite of pronounced cultural diversity,
and in spite of the very divergent teachings and practices
of the new movements, certain very broad trends can be
discerned within the contemporary transformations of
religion.

One feature of the present religious situation although
not intrinsically new is today more impressive than in
earlier times, and that is the extraordinary migration of
religious ideas. Of course, the great world religions all
became very widely diffused from their points of origin,

and some of them flourished better in locales other than those in which they originated—as in the case of both Buddhism and Christianity. But the new cults have spread further and faster, even though some new Christian sects have often travelled along pathways well trodden by earlier and more orthodox Christian missions. Others have found adherents in places and social and cultural conditions far removed from the location of their initial emergence. So we have a world in which Mormonism, which has its main following in Utah, also thrives among the Maori and in Tahiti; in which Jehovah's Witnesses, whose origins are in Pennsylvania, constitute about one and one-half per cent of the total population in Zambia; in which Pente-costalists, who began in Kansas and Los Angeles, form the second largest Church in Sweden. We have a band of devout Muslim Sufis occupying a farm in the Cotswolds; communities of followers of Mr. Sun Myung Moon, the Messianic leader of the movement known as the Unified Family, well established in London and Amsterdam; and practitioners all over America of the severe Kundalini yoga routine of the Sikh leader, Harbhajan Singh (known as Yogi Bhajan), whose faith comes from the Punjab.

The new religious movements are less bound by geo-graphy, less dependent on specific cultures or particular ethnic groups. They draw certainly from particular strata, from among specific publics who are in the statisticians' phrase more 'at risk', but for these publics there is also a wide range of choice. There is a profusion of styles to choose from, and because the new movements have lost their local social base they have much less significance for the social system in which they emerge. Like other leisure-time pursuits, they are a free choice which, providing that the law is not breached, are part of that consumption economy in which men can do, as the modern phrase has it, 'their own thing'. The old correlates of religious dissent —social class, education, and even, in the case of groups like the Hutterian Brethren and the Mennonites, the sheer fact of ethnicity—are no longer so relevant.

The movements that are now growing have emerged at various times in the last century and a half: thus the Mormons are 150 years old; the movement we now know as Jehovah's Witnesses about 100 years old; while Pentecostal sects as such have rarely operated for more than 50 or 60 years. Some showed their greatest growth early; others grew slowly at first to burgeon only more recently. To these groups that have arisen within the Christian tradition, the 'older sects' as they might be called, there are now added others the primary inspiration of which comes from the non-Christian religions. Together they today constitute a highly variegated religious culture. Among the newer movements there is sometimes an observable syncretism as ideas, practices, methods of evangelism, and life-styles have been adapted to their western publics. Nor is the religious milieu the only source for teachings, rituals, and devotional exercises. Some of the new cults have grown up among the disenchanted youth of western countries, and have been open to influence, so that practices deriving from the secular youth culture have sometimes been sanctified by cult leaders and made into new patterns of religious activity. In some cases, movements that began without any conscious religious aspirations have, after a time, discovered that their concerns were really of a religious kind, and that the truths that they propounded or, more typically, the practices in which they engaged were ways of attaining rapport with the supernatural. There is, then, a diversity and a

volatility in the new religious scene that quite surpasses
that of any previous era. Although historians are likely to
think of the multitude of cults in the Mediterranean in the
first and second centuries A.D., or in central Europe in the
early years after the Reformation, or in Britain about
the time of the Civil War, there is really no comparison to
be made. Our modern movements are far more diverse in
style, and draw from a much wider spectrum of the ancient
traditions of many cultures—from therapeutic exercises,
mysticism, meditation, popular psychology, the mass
media, modern science, and even from science fiction—
sources more diverse than anything ever previously known
to man. The speed of transmission is also much greater,
and the possibility of syncretism far transcends that of
even the plurality of gnostic cults of early Christian times.
The numbers involved are also many times greater, and
are drawn from more varied contexts and cultures. The
like of what we now have in religion has never been seen
before.

All religions specify the appropriate procedures for
salvation, but what is taken to constitute salvation is very
variously conceived. It may be the life of the spirit after
death; reincarnation; or resurrection of the body; the
overcoming of evil; release from bodily ills; it may be
narrowly conceived as the attainment of happiness now,
or as the achievement of earthly success. All these forms
of salvation may be found in the world's new religions.
The style of each movement, and the type of clientele that
it attracts, is considerably determined by its particular
soteriological ideas. Every movement seeks to transform the
consciousness of converts, by directing them to salvation
as the supreme goal, and to the prospect of its attainment
through the philosophy, rituals, and moral prescriptions

that it enjoins or by persuading them to open themselves to the new experience that it offers.

Beyond these abstract generalizations lie the diverse specific contents of teaching and practice of these movements, and the different transformations of consciousness which they seek to achieve. These differences are further enhanced by cultural and social variations. The new movements cannot be regarded as one indivisible species: they differ profoundly, even though all of them are engaged in the task of transforming man's interpretation of his world and his destiny. Within the species some broad distinctions may be made, and perhaps the most important distinction lies between the movements gaining ground most dramatically in the Third World and those that are growing in the West.

There are movements in the Third World that may be loosely described as atavistic or nativistic—movements that seek to return men to what are claimed to be older traditions, indigenous practices which offer essentially magical solutions to problems. Most of these movements are local, lacking coherent organization, consistent teaching, and systematic direction, and often they are without any sustained communal activity. What they claim as a restoration of traditional practice is often a hotch-potch of half-remembered rituals, casual innovations, borrowed elements from Christianity, Islam, or some other dominant religious customs.[1] Their appeal is that of locally available spiritual power of an apparently vibrant type. Numerous as they are, no one of them has great significance and they are probably diminishing in number. They belong to a

---

[1] For a discussion of syncretism see Wilhelm E. Mühlmann, *Chiliasmus und Nativismus*, Berlin: Reimer, 1961, and Bryan R. Wilson, *Magic and the Millennium*, London: Heinemann, and New York: Harper and Row, 1973.

phase of cultural contact in which men sought to reject
the present for the past, and in the Third World today the
more vigorous impulse—supported not only by the effect
of education and the mass media, but by the proclaimed
policies of governments and international agencies—is in
the opposite direction. It is not these decreasingly important Third World movements that I wish to take into
account, but rather those which, whatever the differences
that exist among them may be, communicate a new social
ethic. That is to say, they emphasize qualities of personal
integrity, and the transformation of individual consciousness; they prescribe the style of personal relationships;
and they socialize their members into an objective system
of obligation and constraint.

For ease of comparability, let me exemplify these various
new religious movements by taking one from each of three
recognizable types. There are, first, some indigenously
controlled movements that emphasize specific elements of
native culture, even though the principal impetus in their
emergence came from missionaries.[2] Secondly, there are
movements that are inspired by external contacts, but
which have attained local autonomy. And, third, there are
sects in Third World countries that are directed from
western countries. My particular examples are from movements in Zaïre, Chile, and Kenya.

These three movements have relatively little in common,
except that each claims to be Christian and each represents
an effort in the transformation of religious understanding.
In Zaïre (formerly Belgian Congo), there is today a thriving

[2] There are, of course, significant new movements that draw on traditions
other than Christianity, and that are not dependent on missionaries for their
inspiration, particularly among the new sects in Indonesia and the extremely
successful new religions of Japan.

Church known as *L'Église de Jésus-Christ sur la terre par le prophète Simon Kimbangu*. The early history of this Church, which is not our concern here, aroused widespread interest among anthropologists, sociologists, and missiologists.[3] It is enough to recount that Kimbangu was a Baptist catechist in the Belgian Congo in 1920-1. As in the case of some other leaders of new religious movements, Kimbangu found himself without opportunities for promotion in the mission, and perhaps because of this he came to believe in his own prophetic powers. Preaching from the Bible, Kimbangu acquired a reputation both as a healer and as a witch-cleanser—in a society that believed very profoundly in the powers of witchcraft, even though these powers were lightly dismissed by Christian missionaries. Kimbangu's fame spread rapidly and within a few months he was arrested by the District Commissioner, who was alarmed at the disorder caused as people abandoned their work and travelled to see the new prophet who was said to heal the sick and to neutralize the power of witches. Kimbangu escaped, and after some time in hiding gave himself up—entering his native village, mounted on an ass, with his votaries putting palm leaves before his path. The element of imitative drama was sustained by the authorities when, during his trial, and before his conviction, Kimbangu was taken out and flogged. The imagery of martyrdom added to his fame, and although he was sentenced to death, his sentence was commuted and he was kept in prison for thirty years, dying there in 1951. Because his sentence was commuted, natives believed that Kimbangu was too powerful to be killed, and during his

---

[3] For the early history of Kimbangu see Efraim Andersson, *Messianic Popular Movements of the Lower Congo*, Studia Ethnographica Upsaliensia, xiv, Stockholm: Almqvist and Wiksells, 1958.

lifetime he became the focus of a variety of religious movements in the Congo territories of both the French and the Belgians. His name became legendary and was used to legitimate very diverse types of religious activity. Expectations of his return fed messianic ideas. Others invoked his name for semi-political campaigns against the authorities. Several successor-prophets arose celebrating God, Christ, and Kimbangu—a new, locally significant, Holy Trinity. Other 'Kimbanguists' performed traditional, and to westerners, sometimes abhorrent, ceremonies around the graves of the ancestors.

Despite these diverse and inchoate religious impulses, out of the Kimbanguist enthusiasms there emerged, under the direction of three of his sons, a movement that claimed a more specifically Christian inheritance, and which, since the establishment of the independent republic of Zaïre, has grown in the lower Congo into something approximating to a national Church. Despite the emphasis on the Biblical teaching, some western Christians have doubts about the orthodoxy of the Kimbanguist Church. The Kimbangu legends are dubious; uncertainty exists about the exact status accorded to him by the Church authorities; and the Church enjoins a number of specifically African practices that are not easily accommodated into the usual Christian pattern of faith and order. Kimbangu is said to have worked miracles and, according to the 1957 catechism of the Church, he was officially held to have died and been resurrected. Perhaps only those outside the Church have proclaimed him to be the black saviour, the African equivalent of Muhammed or even of Christ, but within the Church he is specifically referred to as the promised Comforter, whom Christians in the West generally regard as the Holy Spirit. It is sometimes claimed that he will return; and that he will participate with Jesus at the Last Judgement; and there is a hint also of a claim to Kimbangu's pre-existence, 'from the beginning'. He is believed to intercede for the faithful with God, and this power is also credited to his earthly wife, Marie Mwilu.[4]

Whether the *Church of Jesus Christ on earth through the prophet Simon Kimbangu* is orthodox or heretical is not my concern, but these claims for the prophet make it clear that the movement diverges considerably from what has normally been taken to be acceptable doctrine among Christians. There are other unusual elements: taboos on pork and on monkey-meat; total prohibition, not only of alcohol, but also of smoking; the significant place that is accorded to dreams and visions; and the designation of the village in which Kimbangu is said to have worked miracles as the new Jerusalem, a place free from witch-craft and suitable for pilgrimage. As in other syncretistic African churches, there is the use, in healings and con-secrations, of holy water, which is carried from N'Kamba, the new Jerusalem, to all distant congregations. Whether the water is thought to be intrinsically powerful or merely symbolic is open to dispute, and perhaps as Kimbanguists grow more sophisticated it will also be subject to reinter-pretation. On the other hand, the Church has not adopted baptism or communion as sacraments, even though the theologians who have pressed the World Council of Churches to recognize the Church have undoubtedly encouraged the Kimbanguists to introduce into their

[4] On the recent development of L'Église de Jésus-Christ sur la terre par le prophète Simon Kimbangu, and for a theological discussion, see Marie-Louise Martin, *Kirche ohne Weisse*, Basel: Reinhardt, 1971 (English translation 1975, *Kimbangu*, Blackwell, Oxford). See also Paul Raymaekers, 'L'Église de Jésus-Christ sur la terre par le prophète Simon Kimbangu', *Zaire* (Revue Congolaise), xiii, 7 (1959), pp. 675–756.

churches a ritual similar to that of communion. Evil spirits and witches are still a preoccupation for the Kimbanguists, and attention is given to revelation in dreams, particularly by the present leader of the Church, who claims to be advised by his deceased father, Kimbangu. Thus elements of mission Christianity are interwoven with elements derived from the indigenous culture. European theologians have urged the Kimbanguist leaders to bring their practice more closely into conformity with that of western Churches: the same theologians also seek to excuse divergences by reference to the strength of indigenous tradition, and by showing that there are parallels between African practice and Old Testament preoccupations.[5]

However unorthodox, the Kimbanguist Church is a powerful agency in the transformation of religious consciousness. If it is capable—under its Christian mentors— of gradually transforming items credited with intrinsic power, such as fetishes, witches, holy water, and ritual acts, after the fashion of magical thinking, into symbolic items, it will have an effect not only on the religious beliefs but perhaps also on the social life of millions. If its exhortations to moral probity are preached and accepted, it will effect the resocialization of its adherents. In providing an African interpretation of Christian salvation, through an African prophet, the Church makes a western tradition into an indigenous tradition. National pride, African identity, Congolese nationhood, are all accommodated in this syncretism. The acceptance of indigenous beliefs, tolerance for indigenous fears and anxieties, is a compromise between the sophisticated Christianity of the advanced West, and the relative ignorance of the African peasant. · It is perhaps one of the few ways in which Christianity

[5] M-L. Martin, op. cit.

can be widely effective in these particular conditions. Nor need modern-day Christians look askance at syncretism, as any historian of the origins of the Christian Church and its practices will readily concede. The Church founded in Kimbangu's name (for he did not found a Church himself) appears to achieve more than the missionaries of the major western denominations. It avoids the identification of religious commitment with political obedience which often occurred with white missionaries in colonial times. It eliminates the rice-Christian. It stimulates ambition in creating leadership roles for local people, for even if the Christian stimulus came from without, the Kimbanguist Church is one of the first *entirely African* large-scale enterprises in this part of Africa.

In the long run, however, Kimbanguism may have another consequence. The transmutation of local magic into symbolic religion; the elimination of fears and tensions about witches; the acceptance of uniform routines and taboos of a utilitarian kind to replace arbitrary local custom—these are all steps towards the eventual diminution of vibrant spirituality. As the invocation of visions and dreams declines, as the drums and the dancing, that so fully correspond to the corporeal sense of reality of the African, diminish in significance, so a less vivid, more verbal, if perhaps more desiccated, Christian faith may follow. And this, as Max Weber has illustrated, is itself a step towards the eventual dominance of the secular.

A movement which is like Kimbanguism in being externally inspired and in having attained local autonomy, but which differs from it in incorporating no extraneous indigenous elements, is the Pentecostal movement in Chile. The close association of landowners, ruling élites, and the Catholic Church in some parts of Latin America gave rise to a popular impression that the continent was monolithic in its religious commitment. In reality considerable unrest has existed, as in the freemasonic, anticlerical, positivist, and spiritualistic movements in Brazil. In other countries, there has been a persistent shortage of priests, and indigenous beliefs have never been eradicated.[6] Yet, whatever the Catholic deficiencies, until the Second World War Protestant missionaries achieved no great success in Latin America. The whole cultural *Gestalt* of the often rather puritanical Protestant denominations stood in sharp contrast to the tolerant, amoral, indolent way of life in many parts of the continent.

After that war a number of American Protestant and sectarian missions began to enjoy increasing success, as indicated by the membership figures of the Mormons, Jehovah's Witnesses, and the Seventh Day Adventists. Statistics for the Pentecostalists are less easily obtained, since, unlike these other movements, they are in fact a congeries of often local, sometimes regional or national, denominations with no one central organization, but all suggest that this fundamentalist, expressive form of Christianity, in which speaking in tongues is a focal point of activity, has become a widespread and vigorous social force in both Brazil and Chile.

Several years ago, a Catholic commentator estimated that about 15 per cent of the population of Chile were Pentecostals, and another suggested that on any given Sunday there was probably a higher proportion of the population participating in Pentecostal services than

[6] See the evidence assembled by Isadoro Alonso, *La Iglesia en America Latina : Estructuras eclesiásticas*, Freiburg, Switzerland, and Bogotá, Columbia : FERES, 1964.

E

attending mass in Catholic churches.[7] My choice of words here, 'participating in Pentecostal services', and 'attending Catholic mass', is deliberate, and may indicate a significant factor in the explanation of the different fortunes of these two Churches. Pentecostalism in Chile has been a very largely grass-roots religion. In contrast to the subservient spectator position of the layman in the traditional Catholic Church, the Pentecostal worshipper was an active, sometimes an initiating, participant.[8] The Holy Spirit was believed to be available in the meeting, and might anoint anyone who had been saved. Exhortation by local preachers, men who were often no better educated than the majority of their listeners, was apparently more effective and more appealing than the ministrations from a remote clerical hierarchy. The Arminian theology of Pentecostalism is implicitly democratic and is well expressed in the words of a popular Pentecostal hymn, 'Whosoever will, may come'. This new style of religious involvement was altogether consonant with the growing democratic ethos of post-war years. The immediate rhythms of simple tunes strummed on a guitar contrasted sharply with formal, solemn, and stately church music, and came to be recognized as 'religious' not by virtue of liturgical purity, but by the enthusiasm that they engendered. Above all, religion was no longer dictated by foreign priests, high dignitaries, and upper classes.

What was also significant in Latin America was the acceptance of religious activity by *men*, who formerly had often regarded religion as a matter mainly for women. In their success as preachers, evangelists, song-leaders, deacons, or as possessors of one or another gift of the

---

[7] On Chilean Pentecostalism see C. A. Lalive D'Epinay, *Haven of the Masses*, London: Lutterworth Press, 1970.   [8] Ibid., pp. 45 ff.

Spirit, men acquired new leadership roles and enhanced status. Many converts were rural people who had migrated to the cities. Those living in the disrupted conditions of rural areas following the breakdown of old-style paternalistic agricultural society found in the Pentecostal sects new fellowship, reassurance, protection, and a reinterpretation of their life-circumstances. Pentecostalism was the basis for the reintegration of community groups. Its expressive emphasis matched the severe emotional disturbance that many people had felt in the breakdown of the older social order, or as they tried to make a new way of life in entirely unfamiliar circumstances. For people who are not themselves very articulate—rural migrants to the city are one example, or Indian native-speakers who must use Spanish to communicate with prospective employers and officials are another—there is perhaps a special symbolic compensatory significance in having the power to speak in unknown tongues, as the gift of the Holy Spirit.

Many of the Pentecostal congregations were organized like an extended family under the patronage of the pastor, whose role became the social equivalent of that of the *patron* in the older type of Chilean social structure. The new *patron* was significant perhaps less for his real power than for his expressive leadership and, because Pentecostalism had a strong ascetic element, for the rigour with which he could induce people to help themselves by living self-disciplined lives. What happens to Pentecostal families in Chile may be achieved by other religions in other countries, but there is no doubt that the acceptance of moral injunctions to abjure alcohol, the new impulse to work in an orderly way, the growing commitment to practise a methodical routine of dedicated service for the movement, and the concern to be a good steward, as the

Bible enjoins—are all important elements in the creation of a new type of man. Pentecostalists appear to attain the moral standards which the movement prescribes and to do so to a far more impressive degree than their Catholic compatriots—even though both Churches make many of the same moral exhortations. Pentecostalism succeeds, perhaps, because exhortation is more democratic encouragement 'one of another', is sustained by more effective processes of internalization, and is less dependent on external, officially prescribed social control, epitomized in particular in the mechanism of the authoritarian confessional. Eventually Pentecostalism may work significant social transformations, if in their meetings Pentecostalists can attain the order and the consistency that all communities require. These are first efforts at consciously remaking social structures for rural people who previously have taken the given collectivities of social life very much for granted, virtually as a part of 'nature'. Those efforts, and the sense of power acquired from organizing social life, may be the beginning of significant processes of social change.

The third type of movement engaged in the religious transformation of the Third World is the western sect. There are many such movements, each differing somewhat from the rest, but some of them engaged in an essentially similar effort at religious conversion. I choose a movement with very different Christian doctrine and practice from either of my previous examples: Jehovah's Witnesses. The central thrust of Witness teaching is the early appearance of Christ on earth to fulfil the promised establishment of God's Kingdom. Their vision is apocalyptic, and the prospect for outsiders is limited. They insist on rules of everyday living which they believe are completely consistent with the Scriptures, and their urgent mission is to publish the word. To this end, they eschew any very considerable involvement with worldly affairs. They do not vote. They dissociate themselves from political and social organizations. They limit their expenditure of time and money mainly to essentials, and they have little interest in the world's pleasures. Their time is pre-empted in work for the cause. Their moral theology is conservative, emphasizing the authority of the man over his wife; the father over the children; work before play; and religion before work. Like many sects, they expel the morally wayward, and expect high standards of probity and dedication.

Jehovah's Witnesses are today found throughout Africa: I choose to examine their effect in Kenya, a country in which they did not effectively begin missionary work until just over a decade ago, when that country was granted independence.[9] Since 1962 the Witnesses have made about 1,200 converts in Kenya, mainly in the larger towns. The evidence of religious transformation from Kenya bears out the intimations already available from other African countries, and particularly from Zambia.[10] (Witnesses in Zambia represent about the same proportion of population as Methodists in Great Britain, but unlike British Methodists Witnesses are socially conspicuous and they are growing.) In African society, Witnesses do become exceptional people. The effect of the severe, almost puritanical, code of morals is evident among them, and although many

[9] My information is based on my own field-work undertaken under a grant from the Social Science Research Council, London. For a fuller discussion see Bryan R. Wilson, 'Jehovah's Witnesses in Kenya', *Journal of Religion in Africa*, 5, 2 (1974), pp. 128–49.

[10] Norman Long, *Social Change and the Individual*, Manchester: Manchester University Press, 1968.

of their moral injunctions are not radically dissimilar from those of other Christian missions their greater effectiveness is apparent.

Kenya, like some other African countries, is dominated by powerful tribal allegiances. Kenyan politicians emphasize the blight of tribalism for the nation, but tribal loyalties remain strong, not least among politicians themselves. Tribal divisiveness has been reinforced by the frequent identifications of particular denominations with specific tribes—a situation that has arisen from the comity agreements made by the early missionaries. The Witnesses have succeeded, however, in elevating their distinctive religious commitment above all other allegiances, whether tribal or national, familial or political. Understandably, this zealous single-mindedness has not endeared the sect to outsiders, but in Kenya, where the official ideology is anti-tribal, their stance can scarcely be faulted. They are perhaps a more effective agency of anti-tribalism than any other.

Witnesses do not undertake any form of social, medical, or general educational work for their Third World converts: they confine themselves to what they regard as the pre-eminently important task—the dissemination of their literature. The convert has no motive for joining the movement except belief, and the movement depends on the inculcation of a powerful, all-embracing religious commitment. It is to this end, as obedience to God, and as a preparation for the moral standards that will be required in the Kingdom of God which they believe is soon to be established on earth, that Witnesses emphasize their moral code.

Kenya is a considerably christianized country, in the sense that the great majority of the population have some nominal attachment to one or another of the denominational missions. Yet what cannot be disputed is that that country, like many others, is beset with a variety of moral problems, which include tribalism, nepotism, corruption, excessive drinking, wife-beating, adultery, and, especially in the cities, violence and theft. To an extent probably greater than that of any of the major denominations, the Witnesses have uniformly instilled principles of moral rectitude into their membership. The greater part of the time spent in meetings is spent in training members to present the message to outsiders, and an important part of that training is personal comportment, regard for others, the lesson of learning how to present oneself in everyday life as a model. The result, of course, is the enhancement of the self-esteem of ordinary rank-and-file Witnesses, and an intensification of self-awareness in the knowledge that they are being judged both by God, with respect to their claim to possess the next world, and by other men, with respect to the fruits of their religion in this one.

The Witnesses in Kenya are above average in education and social standing. Many are men who have come to the cities to make new careers, and for them the success ethic was already part of their orientation to the world, but their new religion, although it demands a great deal of their time, is a powerful reinforcement of that disposition. Witnesses have learned to be punctual, sober (whilst not entirely eschewing alcohol), polite, conscientious, willing, hard-working, thrifty and, above all, to refuse bribes and to remain uncorrupt in their dealings with others, and all this has strengthened their prospects of doing well by the world's standards. The intensity of their commitment appears to have significant consequences for the transformation of individual consciousness and perhaps also, if as yet only incipiently and marginally, for social development. The model of a well-regulated family life, a balanced home budget, stability of relationships between spouses, and the confirmed authority of parents, are all items of importance for the development of a modern type of economic order. Paradoxically, although the Witnesses are concerned essentially with God's coming Kingdom, there are evident unintended social consequences to their operation in everyday contemporary society. In some respects they inherit, albeit with a different theology, the impulses of the Protestant ethic that was disseminated to the merchant classes of Europe through Calvinism, and to the working classes of England through Methodism.

The movements that I have chosen from Third World societies must stand for many others, through which men in many parts of the world are seeking new patterns of meaning, new methods of coping with their anxieties, and new prospects of salvation. From those examples I excluded the atavistic or nativistic movements. I concentrated on what I think are more significant and more numerous groups which, arising in the West, offer prospects of renewal, resocialization, and a new social ethic. These movements are attractive in the Third World, and this even though they make very stringent demands, similar in many respects to the diffusion of the universalistic, utilitarian ethic that arose in the West in the early days of modernization, when social organization was first beginning to transcend the earlier dominance of the local community.

These Third World developments occur at a time when we are all aware of the emergence of new religious movements in the West, but many of the more successful and conspicuous among these movements appear to strike in directions quite contrary to those of the sects in underdeveloped countries. This is not to say that they are nativistic; the return to genuine indigenous pre-Christian traditions is no longer possible. Nor do modern men seeking salvation look towards anything that can be recognizably defined as traditional. If the new movements are in any sense nativistic, it is not local nativism that justifies the use of that term. In their powerful thrust against what might be broadly termed 'the Protestant ethic' and its consequences, they cannot draw on pre-Christian sources, and perhaps not even on sources within our culture that can be regarded as 'pre-secular', but only on sources that are essentially alien and exotic. The new movements in the West do not seek to diffuse a social ethic (even though they may in the wider sense of the term offer an ethic for individuals, or even for communes), but stand over against the demands of existing culture (and perhaps of all cultures), the obligations of which they regard as, if not oppressive, then at least irrelevant to the prospect of attractive salvation. Whereas salvation, even for the sects operating in the Third World, is seen as something associated with a process of creating a new culture and a new society, in the new movements at work in the West the focus is on the individual self or on the self-selected community.

The older sects, which are those that operate so successfully in the Third World, have not gone of course, and some still enjoy considerable success in western countries (the Witnesses and the Mormons most conspicuously), but with very different sections of the population. What we see is continuance of the older sects of the Christian tradition, most conspicuously among relatively unsophisticated people, whose education has been largely traditional and often limited; whilst at the same time there is a growth of new movements among a much more sophisticated, and on average a much younger, population, who have enjoyed a much more worldly experience. Although these new movements diagnose man's problems in diverse ways and offer a range of salvational possibilities, they all depart radically from the soteriological and eschatological prognosis of Christianity.

Traditional Christianity encompassed divergent and not always easily reconciled soteriological themes. It promised men the resurrection of the body at the Last Judgement, or the transmigration of the soul to heaven, or some combination of these possibilities. Although bodily healing and the righteous life in Christian community were also elements of salvation, it was primarily a post-mortem salvation for which life on earth was a preparation.

In recent times Christians have shown less assurance about the nature of life after death, and growing uncertainty about the central truths of Christian salvation. As the Church has become more preoccupied with present life, whether in political, economic, or social terms, it has revealed in a measure just those preoccupations of the new non-Christian sects. Whatever their provenance and whatever the orthodox soteriological teachings of the great traditions to which they are related, the new movements are primarily concerned with the here and now. They promise, whether by a regimen of asceticism or a licence for hedonism, or by some mixture of the two, to increase the happiness and the spiritual power of their devotees in this world and to protect them from the limitations and the baleful influences of everyday life in contemporary society. All of them offer new freedom, new power, a new sense of peace that can be obtained quickly and relatively easily.

Three themes that are by no means mutually exclusive can be readily recognized in the teachings of the new movements: that salvation is gained by becoming acquainted with a special, perhaps secret, knowledge from a mystic source; that ultimate salvation and knowledge comes from the liberation of powers within the self; that real salvation is attained by belonging to a sacred community, whose lifestyle and concerns are utterly divergent from those of worldly people. The first theme, which has some parallels with the Gnostic sectarians of the first and second centuries after Christ, is well represented in Scientology and, at a somewhat different level, in the new magical cults. The second theme typifies most fully the meditation cults, but is also to be found in the numerous quasi-religious movements known as Human Potential movements, and sensitivity-training groups, that have sprung up all over the United States, and which have now begun to establish themselves in London. The third theme is a variant of the monastic ideal, even though today most communities cater for people of both sexes. Groups as diverse as the Unified Family, the Children of God, an extreme Jesus movement, and the cult of Krishna consciousness, all advocate communal living.

Again, one from each of these groups must stand for all the rest—utterly unacceptable as that would be to their votaries, as it is to students of comparative religion. For the sociologist, however, concerned with patterns rather than with specific contents, this may in at least some measure suffice.

The Scientologists are a modern example of groups that might be labelled gnostic. Their belief is that by the study and application of knowledge from a relatively secret, or hitherto inaccessible source, men may obtain hitherto unrealized power to shape their destinies. The basic faith of Scientologists is that by taking a series of courses, the individual can enhance his mental capacity to a point where he can overcome certain psychological blocks that have previously hindered him. Those impediments are believed to have arisen from purely involuntary events or utterances occurring in very early life, or even in pre-natal experience, or indeed in any one of innumerable previous incarnations. They are imprints on the thetan, which might be taken as roughly the equivalent of the soul (although the emphasis is that it is not *within* a person, but is itself a basic reality which 'takes on' a mortal body). Scientology specifies the mental manipulations required to achieve a therapeutic result. It began under the name of Dianetics, and then, following a series of organizational changes, developed into a philosophical and theological system, with a Church and a ministry. The religious aspects of the movement are not conspicuous, however, and Scientology is not exclusive—a believer can continue to be a Jew, a Roman Catholic, or a Muslim.

What Scientology offers the individual is an enhancement of competence with which to deal with the everyday events of life. The benefit is effected by the application of a set of special techniques, which are organized into courses, and which were discovered by L. Ron Hubbard, the movement's leader and founder, in the course of what is claimed to be rigorous scientific research. He prescribed the doctrines, therapeutic techniques, and metaphysical system which constitute Scientology. Hubbard claims to have restored the arcane mysteries of the ancient East and to have made essentially scientific discoveries, which are

---

[11] On Scientology see Roy Wallis, *The Road to Total Freedom: A Sociological Analysis of Scientology*, London: Heinemann (forthcoming).

presented in an argot that has combined the style of both engineering and psychoanalysis. What the individual Scientologist seeks to achieve is the condition known as 'clear'. A clear is a man or woman who, through Scientology, has eliminated all the evil imprints, or engrams as they are called by the movement. By this process his intelligence is enhanced to the point of total and immediate recall of all his life experience, and indeed the experience of earlier lives. The idea of this therapy is to make people more efficient in their everyday activities, although in practice the more successful Scientologists are often recruited into the staff of the organization itself. They become the therapists, *auditors*, who make their livings from the practice of Scientology, and their business is to recruit new members to Scientology courses.

Many aspects of Scientology need not concern us: the extraordinary internal structure of the movement, which is itself thought to be a model of organizational efficiency that will eventually be copied for all human purposes; the complex processes of litigation in which Scientology has been involved; the Government Commissions of Inquiry in Britain, Australia, and New Zealand, and legislation that has curbed the Scientological practice in some countries. Our interest is rather the appeal and impact of a movement which, in two decades, has influenced many thousands of people in the English-speaking world and in Western Europe, promising them a form of salvation unavailable from Christianity.

Scientology offers new power for everyday purposes. It has no more than the vaguest social programme, and little interest in social ethics. (Its own department of ethics is concerned with obedience and efficiency in the movement, not with questions of public morality.) The moral

dispositions of members in their daily conduct in the wider
society is irrelevant, and indeed some Scientological pro-
nouncements about social life echo those of the permissive
age. Discipline is solely directed to the control of teaching
and practice, the maintenance of commitment, and the
concern to recruit new members. Unlike earlier religions,
this movement does not prescribe appropriate behaviour
except as it affects involvement with the movement.

The model for Scientological wisdom is science, even
though Hubbard claims to have picked up all the wisdom
of the East in his colourfully described early life. But there
are other sources of arcane knowledge by which some contemporary men seek salvation. These are various systems
of mysticism and magic. Some of them purport to be 'the
old religion', which existed before Christianity. If that
claim is intended to convey the impression of a widespread
organized cult with a systematic body of theory, it can in
no sense be true. Contemporary magic is an indeterminate
collection of random practices which, although not empiri-
cally verified, are thought to constrain causality. Its sources
range from witchcraft to astrology. Sometimes it is decked
out in metaphysical speculations, embellished with tales
of the miraculous, and elaborated with ritual and symbol. There are some distinctive and recognizable quasi-
metaphysical systems of magic, such as I Ching, Tarot,
Gurdjieffism, but there is also a penumbra of diffuse and
eclectic magical lore. Once magic was part of folklore but
there are few continuities between folklore and contemporary magic in western countries. Magic is now learned
from books and those who practise it are not country folk
but rather an urban public who constitute a cultic fringe
who have often joined, and abandoned, a variety of religious
and magical movements at different times.

Although an analytical distinction may be made between those movements in which salvation is offered through learning a new body of teaching and those in which men are taught to seek to discover new potential within themselves, in practice some cults combine these things. Often the way in which inner capacities are said to be released is by the application of specific techniques. The theoretical distinction is worth maintaining, however, since so many new movements focus on the redemption of the self, by the self, and for the self, that one must take their emergence as itself a significant comment on the ideological individualism of our age, and on the contemporary process of individuation. Their attraction suggests that many people have lost all faith in external systems of knowledge, whether science, political theory, ideology, or religion. The cults suggest that you can save yourself; and no one else, and nothing else, can. They are, in this sense, profoundly anti-cultural movements: not merely are they against the existing culture, but their basic thrust is against *any* culture.

There are too many of these movements to be treated here in any detail—Encounter Groups; Psychosynthesis; Transactional Analysis; Est; Esalen; Primal Theory; Transcendental Meditation (the cult of the Maharishi); and a variety of groups that have been collectively called the Human Potential movement. How many people belong to these movements, in all, is unknown. Some 20,000 people are involved annually in the programmes of one of them, the Esalen centre at Big Sur in California. More than twenty-five distinct groups are operating in the San Francisco area, and it is estimated that more than 17 per cent of the population of that area have been involved with one or another cult of this kind. Far more younger people have been involved than older people, and many who have experience of one cult have also been involved with others. Some estimates suggest that four million Americans have participated in these movements.[12]

Despite variety of technique these groups have much the same message. They teach 'body consciousness', the appreciation of the self as one is now; the art of relaxing; release of the emotions; and the way to avoid what is called 'straight-line thinking'. They offer to rehabilitate the individual without actually changing his quality as a person, by changing nothing more than his attitude to himself. They use techniques of breathing-control, yoga, guided imagery, and role-playing. They tell you that reality is not so hard—it is only your feelings that are hard.

What the movement seeks to overcome is that quality that Americans know as being 'uptight'—that sense of moral indignation which produces censoriousness of others and righteousness about the self. No one perhaps will deny the possible value of a measure of learning about such things. What many may doubt is whether such things need to be communicated through ideas about 'cosmic consciousness' or to be called 'self-actualization', 'species wide synergy', 'unitive awareness', 'transpersonal discipline', or the acquisition of 'ultimate states' to realize ones 'meta-needs'. One may doubt, too, whether such self-actualization can be attained by assertions that:

'Change occurs when one becomes what he is, not when he tries to become what he is not.'

'You are already free—just realize it.'

[12] I have relied for factual information in this and the three following paragraphs primarily on Donald Stone, 'Seeking Transcendence in the Human Potential Movement', a paper read at the Conference on Religious Consciousness in Changing Societies, sponsored by the Institute of Religion and Social Change, Honolulu, 1974.

The emphasis in these movements is on the *here and now* and 'present time'—a concept that is also important in Scientology. The Encounter Groups in particular attempt to undo the individual's sense of social constraint and to make him feel at ease with complete strangers. The method is perhaps to sit together in groups, naked, 'acquiring sensitivity', learning to be aware of one's own body, learning by touching others to regain a sense of contact with life and with people. The process continues in the exploration of each other's bodies, telling everything that one thinks, surrendering privacy, and participating in totally frank discussion. At week-end 'retreats' all over America, and especially on the West Coast, such occasions are now almost routine for many young people, and for some who, youth-envying, are not so young.

Some of these movements have an explicit transcendental reference which others lack, but all of them seek to free the individual from his own mind, from his own emotional restraints—and implicitly from his own culture. There is a continuity in these movements with ideas learned in the inter-war and early post-war years about child-rearing and the dangers of repression. The lesson was perhaps over-learned. Fear of repressing children led to an unwillingness to exercise any control at all over them. The same message has now been learned, or overlearned, with adults: since some people suffer repressive inhibitions, Human Potential groups preach that all inhibition is evil. They specialize in de-inhibiting individuals, and in attacking all the inhibitory mechanisms of society. Increased sensitivity is something of which modern man may stand in need. It is something which a well-brought up child in a stable society might have acquired from the sensitivities that it experienced naturally in a careful home. In an aggressive,

F

competitive, mobile society sensitivity may not be transmitted. However inept, the drastic techniques of the new
cults may be some sort of *cri de cœur* for its reacquisition,
even if the goal they achieve is less the inculcation of moral
concern and disinterested goodwill than the reinforcement
of brash projections of the ego.

These groups clearly possess a strong imprint of American hedonism, an emphasis on present pleasure, and a
denial that the individual need really change in order to
become a vibrant, attractive, and self-realized being. Not
surprisingly, there is a direct continuity between many of
these groups and the drug culture, in which a high proportion of their devotees have been involved: they share the
idea that culture is oppressive and some exponents of the
new techniques talk about the desirability of replacing
'straight-thinking' with 'stoned thinking'. They reject, at
least in theory, the civilized restraints by which men in
developed cultures always live. Inevitably, since those
involved in these movements do not become an open
menace to their fellow citizens, they do not overcome *all*
the inhibitions of everyday life. Somewhere, there is a
continuing dependence on the intimations of conventional
culture about the permitted measure of 'self-realization'.
Yet these cults are a transformation of religion; they
reinterpret the idea of salvation, and their adherents
expect profound changes in the quality of life in a society
in which experience of their techniques becomes widespread.

The third group of new movements emphasizes the
importance of the sacred community as the location of
salvation. Most of them look to the East for the source of
their inspiration, reinterpreting Hindu, Sikh, Muslim, or
Buddhist wisdom, although the new Jesus movement

communities should not go unnoticed. The spiritual exercises of the oriental cults often include yoga, stringent dietetic restrictions, and chanting: and all these movements have, of necessity, regulations for the maintenance of a collective religious life. In contrast with the communitarian Christian sects that settled in America in the eighteenth and nineteenth centuries, the new cults seek new recruits with evangelistic fervour. Unlike the movements that emphasize salvation by self-realization, communitarian movements need a strong sense of their boundaries, and their monopoly of salvation. Whereas those who take up sensitivity training regard their involvements as occasional, the communal cults demand total commitment. To become a member of a commune the individual must prove himself, undergo a period of probation, and become an adept in the movement's spiritual techniques. The community constitutes a total environment, organizing the time, commandeering the resources, and allocating the privileges, and indeed the necessities, of members. In some cases, as in the Unified Family, which claims that its system of divine principles, based on Christian scriptures, have been perfected by their messianic leader, Mr. Moon, and in the Happy–Healthy–Holy Organization (3HO) Sikh communities of the Yogi Bhajan, the individual members may work in employment outside the control of the group.[13] Wages are pooled in a common fund. In contrast, in the

[13] On the Unified Family see Mark Cozin, 'A Millenarian Movement in Korea and Great Britain', *A Sociological Yearbook of Religion in Britain*, 6 (1973), pp. 100-21; and James A. Beckford, 'Two Contrasting Types of Sectarian Organization', unpublished paper delivered at VIIIth World Congress of Sociology, Research Committee for the Sociology of Religion, Toronto, 1974. On the Happy–Healthy–Holy Organization I have relied upon Alan Tobey, 'New Errand into the Wilderness: the Summer Solstice of the Happy–Healthy–Holy Organization', a paper read to the Conference on Religious Consciousness (see note 12 above).

Hare Krishna movement, a member devotes all his time to working in and for the community.

Understandably, these movements emphasize group consciousness rather than the realization of the self or that self can be realized only within the group. Obviously, not all adherents can be inducted into communal life immediately. Equally, a movement needs outside support, and the movements often need the services of people whose worldly involvements continue to be essential for group growth. Thus there is often an order of primary members, *religious*, in the community centres or ashrams, and a second order of as yet unincorporated members outside, some of whom are probationers for communal life.

The Divine Light Mission of Maharaj Ji illustrates the style of these new movements that build up the idea of salvation in the sacred community. Not all devotees belong to ashrams but in the United States about 4 per cent do engage in full-time mission work. Members are celibate, vegetarian, non-drinkers, and non-smokers.[14] They promise obedience and do whatever work is assigned to them in their spare time. They have outside jobs, and they contribute money and their spare-time work to the Mission. In addition to the ashrams there are 'Premie Centers' for married, non-celibate couples—a 'household' of devotees who may be as many as thirty people. They give 30 per cent of their household income to the Mission. Devotees are thus inclined, and even encouraged, to draw together as a community. The ashrams and centres support *Divine Sales* outlets and *Divine Services*. How the organization is

[14] On the Divine Light Mission I have relied on Jean Messer, 'Divine Light Mission', to appear in a forthcoming study on religious consciousness edited by Robert N. Bellah and Charles Y. Glock, and to be published by the University of California Press.

financed is not clear, but adherents believe in divine grace as the source of their needs. There are as in many such movements many stories of miracles of divine provision.

The real focus of salvation in the Divine Light Mission is meditation. The Maharaj Ji offers perfect knowledge.

The Kingdom of Heaven is within you. And I can reveal it to you.

The Maharaj Ji, who is now sixteen or seventeen, claims perfect Masterhood, offering perfection to others and offering contact with Divine Energy. God is the unifying force of the cosmos and the individual can know *God* directly. His devotees 'receive knowledge', through a *mahatma*: of whom Maharaj Ji has about 2,000—all from India or Tibet. Knowledge is said to come in a knowledge session, and be experienced as an intense light which is seen in meditation, as a special sound, as a special taste, and as an inner vibration. All these sensate experiences are achieved by the initiate relatively early in his career in the movement, and without special ritual. The experience is recognized as addictive—devotees thirst for it. The knowledge is gained in meditation, in even greater measure than in the knowledge sessions, or at *Sat Sung*, the occasions for discussion among devotees about their spiritual experiences. What is claimed is a strong sense of personal guidance in everyday life, a sense of God's love, for God is loving, benevolent, and playful. The Mind is the hindrance to knowledge since knowledge comes from experience. This, then, is not prayer but meditation—seeing, hearing, tasting, and feeling God, even though all these things appear to be beyond the possibilities of the actual senses. This religion is thus not concerned with specific beliefs or moral precepts: knowledge is within: it is realized by meditation and the Divine Light Mission is a way of helping others to realize it. Listening to others in the *Sat Sung* is also a way of 'getting high' as it is sometimes put, of achieving happiness. And as happiness is manifested, so others will be impressed and get the chance of true knowledge. Devotees believe that they have met God and in their gratitude they accept all the demands of the Divine Light Mission. This movement is thus in no sense inter-dictive, it is not primarily ascetic nor dogmatic, nor concerned to disseminate an ethic. There are no apparent constraints to deter the prospective member. Maharaj Ji says:

Give me your love and I will give you peace. Give me the reins of your life and I will give you salvation.

It is perhaps not surprising that some of his followers see him as the promise of Revelation though this is not the primary claim made by him or for him.

The Hare Krishna movement is perhaps *par excellence* the movement emphasizing salvation in the community. Krishna Consciousness began as a western movement in 1966, when A. C. Bhaktivedanta Swami, who claimed a direct link with Krishna, travelled from India to establish the American version of what he claimed to be ancient Indian religious discipline. The intellectual source of the movement was Bhaktivedanta's own interpretation of the *Bhagavad Gita*. The ideal of discipline for adherents was to be complete insulation from the outside world, by shaving the head, donning the saffron robe, and under-going a six-month probation period for acceptance into a residential community as a full member.[15]

[15] Information on the Krishna Consciousness movement is from Clarence H. Snelling and Oliver R. Whitley, 'Problem-Solving Behaviour in Religious

The movement's headquarters was changed from New York to San Francisco after a short time and there, in the area of Haight-Ashbury, the centre of hippy culture, the new cult found recruits. It deliberately sought to attract these young people with slogans such as:

Stay High forever
No more coming down: practice Krishna Consciousness.

The images that were employed—the expansion of consciousness; cleaning the dust from the soul by chanting; the experience of vibrations—all indicate the significant continuities of concepts already well established in the drug culture. Prospective followers were urged to 'Turn on: tune in: drop out of movements employing false states of consciousness' and most of all to drop out from involvement in the wider society.

Krishna Consciousness rejects logic and rational argument as false trails in the search for true freedom and happiness: only the teacher, the book (the *Gita*), and the experience were held to be valid. The material world is rejected, since what really matters is the mind of the individual, and that mind can be freed from false concerns by the practice of Bhakti-yoga discipline, which alone can lead the individual to eternal bliss. No other knowledge is necessary, nor even desirable. Education, worldly concerns, material possessions can all be abandoned, since the only worthwhile thing is the consciousness of Krishna. In so far as the movement has a vision of the future, of

and Para-Religious Groups', in Allan W. Eister (editor), *Changing Perspectives in the Scientific Study of Religion*, New York: Wiley, 1974, pp. 315-34; and from Gregory Johnson, 'A Counter-Culture in Microcosm: Sources of Commitment to the Hare Krishna', to appear in R. N. Bellah and C. Y. Glock (editors), op. cit. See also Irving I. Zaretsky and Mark P. Leone, *Religious Movements in Contemporary America*, Princeton: Princeton University Press, 1974.

a new age of peace and love, it is a future to be achieved only by the dissemination of Krishna consciousness to everyone.

In the temple, a *wholly-other* conception of the world is presented by a powerful onslaught on the senses, through music and chanting, incense, exotic paintings, and the use of Sanskrit, an unknown language to new western converts. These sense impressions are apparently more important than the actual teachings of the *Gita*: experience counts for more than mere intellectual knowledge. It is to experience that the self is to surrender. In shaving the head, taking the robe, changing the name, the individual's self-conception is transformed symbolically, as the basis for a further resocialization to the norms of the community. Poverty, the abandonment of material possessions, the acceptance of a vegetarian diet, and the renunciation of personal gratifications (such as the use of intoxicants and drugs, and of sexual relationships outside marriage) are the things that are required of a committed devotee. Pleasure is to be sought only in the service of Krishna.

The asceticism of this movement is not that of medieval ascetics. The emphasis is on self-realization, and the means are not service of the wider society on *its* terms, but service of the Krishna community on terms that are deviant from general social norms, that are indeed counter-cultural. Modern young people have learned about 'the presentation of the self in everyday life', and they know about the manipulation of one's image. They have a self-awareness of a kind quite different from any that has existed in previous periods of history. Since it is so easily subjected to manipulation, even the self is not to be trusted in the modern world. For people who have absorbed, albeit unconsciously, intimations of this kind, the exotic quality of Krishna Consciousness presents a simple challenge to honesty in terms uncompromised by the institutionalized corrosions of received Christianity. It is radical because the cultural appurtenances of everyday life have to be given up. It is reassuring because it offers stable community life in a world of inchoate aspirations and permanent mobility and change. It facilitates new beginnings because it rests on entirely alien premisses. Yet it does all this without losing significant continuities with deviant sub-cultures, particularly the experience of drugs. It represents a more total rejection of the society with which the young are disenchanted than the occasional leisure-time recourse to drugs, yet it sustains an attractive, almost a hallucinatory other-worldly appeal.

Communitarian living requires discipline, and in this respect the Hare Krishna cult offered a new basis of authority—that of the committed group; and in this it is in contrast with the complete subjectivism and normlessness of the drug experience. Ecstasy now became regularized and almost predictable through the use of a mantra by which the objective culture might be denied. A new language made apparent the significance of group reinforcement for the individual's own experience, and the community became the only context and the only criterion by which to define reality. Like other total institutions, this cult de-individuated its members, putting them into uniform and imposing restraints on individual attachments. The drill of communal chanting was a routinization of personal ecstasy, canalizing but also draining the individual's emotions in this standard process of release. By providing boundaries—even for a generation that had become distrustful of all boundaries and all forms of discrimination—the Krishna community located subjective experience in a context of security. None the less, routinized ecstasy and regulated euphoria raise their own problems. No on-going societal (as distinct from communal) culture can be based on such experience, even though, for a limited time and in particular conditions, small insulated communities that are parasitic on the wider society may sustain themselves.

The new missions to old believers, as I have called the plethora of modern cult movements in both the western world and in developing countries, are as yet an incalculable force in the process of religious and social change. Some will undoubtedly disappear. Others will themselves undergo transformations as they cope with new cultural situations and the exigencies of external change. Three things appear to threaten these movements in the longer run: the first, which is the very factor that has facilitated their initial success, is the absence of social stability in the wider society; the second is their own frequent lack of effective agencies for the socialization of a second generation of believers; and the third, their incapacity for integration with the dominant agencies of the increasingly secular societies in which they operate. It is easy to become a devotee of a new religion when one is only relatively loosely attached to the wider social system—and this applies to the new and as yet unsettled urban migrants in Africa or Chile, as well as to young people without dependants or stable life commitments in western society. As yet, sectarians in the Third World may, by social and vicinal segregation, and their great community integration, retain their second generation, but their relation with the political, education, and other authorities remains uncertain. In the west, while social integration is not desired by the cults, diverse forms of religious deviation may persist without interference as long as they can support themselves, but for most adherents there is a problem about the continuing commitment of their kin. Many of these movements are highly individualistic, which in itself militates against their faith being carried along the lines of family association. Others, though communal, make poor or socially unacceptable provision for the routine social life of children. Individual involvement with any of these movements is inclined to be ephemeral, and movements with high turnover rates tend to evolve strategies of recruitment that devote little time to the induction of children into the, often transient, faith of their fathers.

If these things are true, there must be profound consequences both for religion and for its influence on society. Hitherto, religious groups have generally become institutionalized within a stable social system, purveying what were regarded as eternal truths, appropriate to be handed on from father to son. Even though technical change occurred, and even though the structure of society was amended, moral wisdom was assumed to have a timeless validity. In recent generations the effects of very rapid social change have been to challenge, not so much the intrinsic truth of received morality, as the possibility of applying it in societies that are organized by the relatively impersonal interaction of role performers, each of whom plays his segmented part in the more mechanical operation of the whole. Perhaps not surprisingly, we see the contemporary emergence of vigorous anti-moral movements even among those movements that regard themselves as 'religious'.[16] These movements emphasize hedonism,

[16] On the Church of Satan in San Francisco see two papers by Marcello Truzzi, 'Witchcraft and Satanism', and Edward J. Moody, 'Urban Witches', in Edward Tiryakian (editor), *On the Margin of the Visible: Sociology, the*

the validity of seeking present pleasure, the abandonment of restraint, and an ethic of 'do your own thing'. In the past religion was a primary socializing agency of men, teaching them not only new rituals but something of the seriousness of eternal verities. From a sociological perspective, those verities were not specific doctrines about deities and spirits, but were the irrefragable facts of conflict, evil, suffering, and death. Through myth and symbol, religion offered men not ways of overcoming the ineluctable but ways of coming to terms with it. Death conditioned life rather more then than we in our age should wish to accept. Suffering was more readily tolerated than a scientific generation feels either necessary or desirable. But in the end, what was offered was a reconciliation of man to circumstance. Such reconciliation, many thought, would in the future be achieved by science, but in a rapidly changing world we now know that men will never really be reconciled to circumstances. Such a conclusion was never attainable, but the hope for it was socially important: today we have lost the agencies that gave us even the hope of reconciliation.

In the transmission of religious commitment from father to son there was inevitably also the transmission of a cultural constraint, powerful indications of what was to be done. Religion was the vehicle of culture, providing men with guidelines for life together. Man has devised no other institution for this function, and it may be doubted whether, by later-life training in sensitivity enhancement groups, men can ever make up for that natural sensitivity which in

Esoteric, and the Occult, New York: Wiley, 1974. The Church of the Final Judgement (formerly known as 'The Process'), which has members in Britain, the United States, and Canada, recognizes Satan and Lucifer, as well as Jehovah, as deities to be worshipped.

a stable society at its best might be transmitted by gentler and better-sustained, better-integrated processes of education, parental care, and spiritual guidance. If future religions are not to be institutionalized, but are to be as ephemeral as each generation, one powerful force for civilization will be lost to man, and there may not be adequate new devices to function in its stead.

III

The Social Meaning of Religious Change

IT would be aesthetically gratifying if one could point easily to a set of trends at work within contemporary religion and to some corresponding set of changes in society, and indicate convincingly the relationships between these two groups of phenomena. In the nature of the case, however, all that can be done is to establish the broad conditions within which both secularization and the emergence of new movements have occurred. For the sociologist, it is axiomatic that the sources of change in religion should be looked for primarily in the social system. At one time, processes of religious change, in so far as they were recognized at all, were interpreted by believers in essentially religious terms. Thus it was that when a religious revival occurred in eighteenth-century North America, it was seen by men like Jonathan Edwards as the work of God, as the Spirit moving the waters of human consciousness. But even by the mid nineteenth century eminent Christians were looking for social rather than divine causes of religious change. Charles Finney, the revivalist, made it clear in his celebrated lectures on revival that it was not necessary to wait for God to stir the minds of men: if a revival was wanted, then there were appropriate rational steps that men could take in order to produce one.[1] His own revival

[1] C. G. Finney, *Lectures on Revivals of Religion*, 1835.

campaigns were seen as a consequence of serious human planning, and not merely as an evidence of God's grace. Here then was an early Christian recognition that spiritual consequences had social, and sometimes conscious, causes.

This contention does not rule out the possibility that religious changes may themselves have profound social consequences, and, as my discussion of new movements in Zaïre, Chile, and Kenya indicates, it is evident that new movements like these, becoming institutionalized, are pregnant with possibilities for their own communities and for the wider societies within which they develop. The new movements in the West, however, which lack a tendency to become integrated with the wider society, may have consequences that are much more confined in time and space to the self-selected groups of votaries who either drop out of society into these relatively encapsulated groups or use religion as little more than a convenient personal therapy in their leisure hours. Since, in many cases, these movements are profoundly anti-cultural, to the point sometimes of accepting assertions that they constitute a 'counter-culture', any institutional integration with the wider society is not to be expected. Their prospects for creating an alternative culture is something that we must examine below.

In discussing contemporary transformations of religion, I have concentrated on two issues: secularization and the decline of old faiths; and sectarianism, the rise of new cults. It seems entirely to be expected that, as old religious institutions lose their social significance and as old beliefs appear culturally less and less credible to more and more people, new, often highly specialized, religious cults should come into being. They offer new therapies, new access to power, new modes of personal reassurance, and occasionally, though with less emphasis and more vagueness, even suggest something like a new social order. The idea of a new sort of society is rarely more than the expectation that as a new therapeutic style is diffused, so, in unspecified ways, social institutions will adapt in conformity to it. Few outside these movements can believe that the contemporary social system is quite so vulnerable, or so readily influenced either by the self-chosen life styles of enclosed cult communities, or by the spread of therapeutic play activities among citizens on week-end retreats at sensitivity-training centres.

Although some variants of Christianity still flourish in the Third World, secularization is the dominant feature of contemporary religious change in the West. Christians have responded to secularization in various ways, five of which may be readily distinguished, and summarily designated as: ecumenism; charismatic renewal; voluntary destructuration; rationalization; and eclecticism. The partially failed hopes of ecumenism have already been mentioned. Charismatic renewal has also been discussed above, although some of the following comment on the last three of these responses also apply to that movement.

Voluntary 'destructuration', to use the term fashionable among sociologists, is the deliberate process of abandoning old forms and procedures. The term encompasses developments such as the abandonment of the Latin Mass in the Roman Church; experimentation with secular symbols in the liturgy of many churches; the rejection of hierarchy; the encouragement of sacramental performances by laymen; the ordination of women (in the Swedish Lutheran Church, for example). Destructuration is an attempt to accommodate the Church not only to the fluidity of contemporary society, but even to the vociferous pressure

G

groups that dominate the mass media and that impress the contemporary public with the false dichotomy that everything not utterly modern is necessarily completely out of date. Thus, beliefs, rituals, even moral precepts are relinquished. The new styles in music, in dress (or undress), are largely influenced by the entertainment industry, as if, backhandedly, churchmen acknowledged the competition of the media for man's leisure time as the determining consideration of their own presentation of themselves and of the faith. Thus it is that the sphere of the sacred is surrendered to the intrusions of the secular: this process is not the conquest of the world by the faith, but the conquest of the faith by the artful techniques of the world.

Paradoxically perhaps, the attempts to *de*-structure the Churches is not out of accord with the styles and sentiments of the Charismatic Renewal movement, which also attempts to cut through formal routines. In both developments one may observe the imprint of contemporary social moods. The demand to see religion 'working', engendering emotions, making men do things (even if those things are not of great social consequence in themselves), reflects the emphasis in contemporary sales techniques. The call for speed displaces slow but tested methods at all levels of social life, in education as in our exchange of tranquillizers for set patterns of well-regulated rounds of familiar activities. The old idea of learning, of a steady habilitation, of socialization, of necessarily recurrent dedication to God, 'each returning day', is set aside for religion by rapid results. The change is entirely in conformity to the pressure of contemporary society. The idea of steady growth in grace, perhaps of a lifelong cultivation of understanding, is replaced by the modern demand for instant access to authentic reality. The authenticity is guaranteed by subjective feeling, reinforced by group-engendered emotions, for the reality is to be felt rather than realized cognitively or learned by habituation to orderly procedures. Feeling is quick: but spiritual and intellectual cultures are slow. It almost seems as if some churchmen have learned and applied the advertising slogans for credit cards that promised to 'take the waiting out of wanting', and have decided to take the waiting out of 'waiting on God'.

Throughout western society, the younger generation of the 1960s were repeatedly told by the new interpreters of the younger Marx, by Herbert Marcuse, and by Mao, that the objective structures of western society were themselves an enslaving system of alienation. The message fed the subjectivism of the drug culture, and was confirmed by the widely acclaimed failure of western politicians. The 'credibility gap' between politicians and their publics appeared to apply no less to religion. As authority was disputed, so all the objective systems of society were brought into disrepute—the very agencies by which, until recently, justice, knowledge, faith, and social decencies were themselves authenticated. New procedures based on modern radical-democratic principles have had profound consequences for the Churches, as for education, and potentially for law. But religion is a more vulnerable social institution than education, and is more susceptible to the demands of a clientele. It is perhaps not surprising that even more readily than education, the priests have acquiesced in the changing balance of power, as they saw it. From being custodians of morality, many of them have gladly surrendered their uncertainties about the faith and its social prescriptions, in order to engage in 'dialogue' (is it mandatory to refer to it as 'meaningful dialogue'?) with the people. Perhaps implicit in the democratization of the

Churches is the new faith that virtue resides especially in the lowest classes, it comes up from below, from the least educated, the least socially favoured, whether they be seen as the working classes, or as ethnic minorities, or even as delinquent groups.

If religion has been more affected by this social current than other institutions, this is largely because of the failure of the fourth of the five responses to the contemporary situation that I mentioned above. That response, rationalization, approximates a process known to sociologists as *co-optation*. Faced with secularization, itself largely the result of the rationalization of social procedures, some churchmen believed that, since rationalization could not be defeated, the best course for the Church was to espouse it. Secularization is in large part intimately involved with the development of technology, since technology is itself the encapsulation of human rationality. Machines, electronic devices, computers, and the whole apparatus of applied science are rational constructs. They embody the principles of cost efficiency, the choice of the most effective means to given ends, and the elimination of all superfluous expenditure of energy, time, or money. The instrumentalism of rational thinking is powerfully embodied in machines.

If rationalization of procedures has been the dominant course of recent history, and if secularization has occurred because of this process, it could be expected that the Church should respond by seeking to rationalize its own operations, in conformity with the thinking of the times.[2]

[2] The best-known advocate of rationalization in the Anglican Church is Leslie Paul, *Deployment and Payment of the Clergy*, London: Church Information Office, 1964. For a critical review see Bryan R. Wilson, 'The Paul Report Examined', *Theology*, lxviii, 536, pp. 89-103. See also Leslie Paul, *A Church by Daylight*, London: Chapman, 1973.

Up to a point the Church has done this: some operations, particularly the financial investments on which both the Anglican and Roman Churches so largely depend, are under the control of separated agencies which, no doubt, conform in their activities to the rational economic assumptions of the market. But in other respects the attempts to rationalize have been spasmodic, partial, and subject to compromise. The reason is that religious concerns are themselves ultimately not reducible to the rational. Religious activity is for its own sake: its end is the glory of God and the salvation of men. It has no empirical product, no objective tests. Its procedures cannot, therefore, be subjected to any consistent process of rationalization. Western religion has been deeply concerned with moral matters, with the quality of relationships, but these relationships are themselves between persons, not between role-performers: they are not subject to rational order.

Just as religious faith defies rationalization, when its proponents retreat into declaring some propositions to be a 'mystery', to be apprehended only by faith, so religious institutions also show a low capacity for rationalization. The basic reason for this is that religion is always primarily a communal, as distinct from a societal, institution. Its operation is always essentially local. The basic commodity that religion purveys—reassurance about salvation—must be available wherever its agents operate. The vital activities to reassure men must be replicated over time and space. Unlike economic organization, or law, or education, within which institutions a rational, societal hierarchization can be established, religion is limited in its internal subdivisions. Whereas to obtain higher levels of legal enactment or jurisdiction, or educational provision, the individual must have recourse to more central agencies, the Church, at least with respect to its ultimate concern, must be, or claim to be, equally effective in all localities. Every local agent must have adequate competence as a purveyor of the commodity with which the Church is concerned. Thus, even though as a political structure a Christian Church may be hierarchic, because religion deals in an indivisible ultimate, man's need for reassurance about salvation, so the principle of hierarchy is overborne by the need for an even diffusion of agents of adequate competence.

It follows that a religious institution cannot embrace the principle of rationality either in its teachings or its organization. If so much of man's recent endeavour has been to create a rational social order and a rational technical system, then it cannot be otherwise than that the Churches will find themselves increasingly at odds with other institutions, and increasingly at a disadvantage in ordering their affairs, since they cannot avail themselves of the fruits of what is generally regarded as social and technical progress. The modern world operates on essentially instrumental principles, but the Church must be concerned with ultimate ends, and not with the relative efficiency of means. The moral embedded in the question, 'What man of you, having an hundred sheep, if he lose one of them doth not leave the ninety and nine . . . and go after that which is lost?' is not a moral that can be defended on the rational principles that govern the modern world.

The fifth response of the Churches is most evident in the United States. What I have called *eclecticism* is an attempt to incorporate into worship elements from other cultures and subcultures, or from other social contexts.

One example of it has been in the attempt to embrace political issues, where particular sections of the ministry have had reason to suppose that their potential clientele were really more interested in politics than in worship. The Vietnam war provided the occasion, and the university campus the locale, for a vigorous attempt to politicize religion on the part of that section of religious professionals known as 'campus clergy'. These ministers responded to their clientele, and no doubt influenced them further, in a variety of protest marches and demonstrations, and we know that, within the ministerial profession, the campus clergy were considerably over-represented statistically in enterprises of this kind. At that moment, politics provided an opportunity for action that attracted modern men, and modern ministers, much more than the slower work of the cure of souls of a less-youthful population.[3]

Politics has not, however, been the primary source of new engraftments for religious action. Entertainment, the so-called 'counter-culture', and other religions have contributed more. Some American seminaries have developed these new concerns, offering to train the clergy in 'the new culture'. Ministers must now acquire new styles, and learn to manipulate their image to conform to the requirements of a new generation. Worship is to be regarded as play, and individuals should be free to choose their own way of worshipping. This makes the Church into a place of experimentation, not a place of prescriptive conformity. So the minister is expected to be open-minded about yoga, to encourage classes in new techniques of breathing, to sponsor rock festivals, and to promote classes in radical politics. Meditation and sensitivity-training are things that a modern minister should know about, in order to

[3] See P. E. Hammond and R. E. Mitchell, op. cit.

encourage those who are interested in these things to embark on just this type of spiritual exploration.[4]

Thus, religion is divested of its former culture-subserving function: the demands of traditional culture, received courtesies, common decencies of the past, are almost regarded as stultifying the individual's spiritual growth. Those demands were, after all, only the parochial preoccupations of Christianity. Modern men have acquired a knowledge that transcends these local cultural demands of the oppressive local community. There are other cultures that are attractive because they are exotic. Christianity can be regarded as that religion that just happens to be the received tradition of our culture. With more extensive knowledge of a wider world, Christianity is relativized; its ordinariness is exposed. The new eclecticism proposes to supply its deficiencies from more vibrant sources of exotic power.

The new eclecticism, brooking no organizational restraints, carries the spirit of ecumenism further and faster. Perhaps its most vigorous exponent is the Harvard theologian, Professor Harvey Cox. Mr. Cox was one of the more prominent 'secular theologians' of the early 1960s. At that time, he rejoiced in the fact that Christianity was producing secular man, man come of age: 'religion' at that time was, for him, a dirty word. Christianity was to be 'religionless'.[5] In recent years, Mr. Cox has rediscovered, if not his faith, at least his interest in faith; and this he has done by espousing the youth culture and its new religious style.

[4] An account of new strategies in American churches is provided by James S. Wolfe, 'A Kick in the Bastion: The Impact of the Counter-culture on Protestant Congregations', a paper delivered at the Conference on Religious Consciousness, Institute of Religion and Social Change, Honolulu, 1974.

[5] Harvey Cox, *The Secular City*, New York: Macmillan, 1965.

Mr. Cox advocates the global religious commune, in which all kinds of celebration may occur simultaneously.[6] 'Liberation' is the watchword, and people are to be liberated by being induced to tell their own stories, which becomes an agency of salvation. The world is divided into the self-indulgent and playful men of righteousness on the one hand, and those who reject spontaneity, cultivate inhibitions, and who are in the modern phrase 'uptight', on the other. Salvation, it appears, is attained by learning to indulge oneself.

The influence of the theories that sustain Esalen and the sensitivity-training cults of the United States is evident. But Mr. Cox is not merely a theorist. As a Baptist minister he has opportunities to explore new forms of celebration. For a Baptist, he is a convert to ritual, not merely to the rituals of branches of Christianity older than his own denomination, but to virtually any religious ritual.

The symbolic treasures of the full sweep of human history are available to us, everything from the oldest cave drawing to the newest image of Utopian hope.[7]

Fiestas, therapies, chants, light shows, dances—all are legitimate material to incorporate into liturgy, since all may help to unlock the hidden recesses of the psyche, which in itself is, for Mr. Cox, a process of salvation. In one exercise in 'experimental liturgics', Mr. Cox organized a ritual celebration for Easter. The place was a Boston discothèque, a location in which such a ritual had no local cultural significance. The basic rite was to be Byzantine, a form which, however traditional in itself, had no bearing on local tradition. But this was only the basis for other elements.

[6] See Harvey Cox, *The Seduction of the Spirit*, London: Wildwood House, 1974.   [7] Ibid., p. 243.

We wanted to surround the colourful Byzantine . . . Mass with participatory liturgical dance . . . with light-and-music collages, with physical encounter movements—and also somehow to bring those powerful Old Christian symbols of New Life and shared bread more directly into the service of human liberation.[8]

Nearly two thousand people participated. They painted peace signs, crosses, fishes, and assorted graffiti on each other's faces and bodies. With silver paper crowns they crowned each other. They painted on long strips of paper attached to the walls. Scenes of war and death were then projected, and in turn were interrupted by 'free-wheeling liturgical dancers dressed in black and white leotards', who enticed people 'into sacred gesture and ritual motion'.

People who had never danced in their lives stretched out arms and flexed legs and torsos. The lithe solemnity of the movements made me think we should get rid of pews for ever. . . . In one group a teeny began humming 'Jesus loves me' and soon her whole arm-and-leg enmeshed group began to hum with her.[9]

Choruses from Bach's 'St. Matthew Passion', a gospel reading, Handel's 'Hallelujah Chorus', followed. There was jumping, hugging, and moaning, and then communion was celebrated by a Roman Catholic priest, an Episcopalian, two ministers of the United Church of Christ, and Mr. Cox. People then chanted the Hindu mantra, *Om*, and fed each other the communion elements. The kiss of peace 'was not just a discreet peck on the cheek'.[10] Finally, to a record of the Beatles singing 'Here comes the sun', they rushed out to greet the sunrise, chanting.

Whatever else such an event indicates, it makes manifest

[8] *The Seduction of the Spirit*, p. 156.   [9] Ibid., p. 157.
[10] Ibid., p. 163.

the disenchantment with the received Christian tradition, which is clearly not regarded as enough, and which may be regarded as counter-productive for those seeking salvation through liberation. In such an experimental liturgy, each exotic bauble is divorced from its context, from its cultural significance, is wanted only for its brightness, to deck out a jollification. The strange symbols are not wanted for their quality as solemn communicators of values, but only as titillations for jaded palates that have experienced too much, too quickly, and too lightly. Without any sustained knowledge, without any awareness of what symbols stand for, of what choices have to be made, of what discriminations are imperative to culture and to human life, these modern men demand everything. Modern communications have produced a new liturgical emporium, from which all items may be carelessly and mindlessly brought together, not to represent an appreciation of the accumulated inheritance of past culture, but merely so that a few people may be *high* for an hour or two. Ecstasy is, of course, an element in religious tradition, but it is never one that has the greatest long-run consequence, until momentary ecstasy is transformed into the lifetime of grace.

The various responses of churchmen and theologians to the dual challenge of secularization and the new sectarianism are ambivalent, equivocal, oscillating, and in part contradictory. Although Christianity has itself been an agency that promoted the incipient processes of secularization and rationalization, yet there is a point beyond which no religious system can go in the adoption of secular and rational strategies. On the other hand, Christians must reject the total commitment to complete mysticism and communal withdrawal of many of the new cult movements, and must also reject the message of complete self-indulgence and liberation which constitute the message of the sensitivity-training groups.

The scope, scale, and pervasiveness of secularization make it the more serious challenge to traditional religion, but there are sociologists who profess to see in the growth of new cults important evidence that controverts the hypothesis that has become known as 'the secularization thesis'. For them, the new cults represent religious revival.[11] In contrast, I regard them as a confirmation of the process of secularization. They indicate the extent to which religion has become inconsequential for modern society. The cults represent, in the American phrase, 'the religion of your choice', the highly privatized preference that reduces religion to the significance of pushpin, poetry, or popcorns. They have no real consequence for other social institutions, for political power structures, for technological constraints and controls. They add nothing to any prospective reintegration of society, and contribute nothing towards the culture by which a society might live.

The religious revivals of earlier times were not of this kind. They had significant social consequences. They occurred in societies with basic units of much smaller scale, when the diffusion of new dispositions, and the inculcation of new attitudes were vital adjuncts in the process of social change—as in the Third World they may be still. The West, in contrast, appears to have passed beyond the point at which religious teaching and practice can exercise formative influence over whole societies, or any significant segment of them. The new cults cannot be

[11] Conspicuous among those who argue in this way is Andrew M. Greeley, *The Persistence of Religion*, London: SCM Press, 1973.

compared with Methodism, which some scholars have
regarded as so important that they credit it with the preven-
tion in England of the equivalent of the French Revolution.
Methodism arose at a time when society was still largely
regulated by personal relationships, and could thus affect
social structure by mobilizing individual dispositions.
What it accomplished was a massive gentling of the people:
new values were communicated, and standards of disinterested goodwill were steadily diffused through a much
wider body of the population.

In developing nations, western movements still organize
men into stable communities and elicit from them high
levels of personal commitment. Although local magic,
witchcraft, and cultism still exist, the movements of transformation gain ground, disseminating new standards of
self-dependence, personal integrity, autonomy, and disinterested commitment. Movements as different as Pentecostalism in Chile, the Kimbanguist Church in Zaïre,
Witnesses, Mormons, and Seventh-Day Adventists in
many parts of the developing world appear to achieve
some of the same social consequences that Methodism
once achieved in England. In all these cases there are
prospects of the resocialization of previously demoralized
local communities.

Neither past revivalism in western countries, nor contemporary transformations in developing nations, can be
likened in their effects to the new exotic cultism and
eclecticism in the modern West. We have already noted
that in western society men have become role-performers
in a system that demands the performance of roles before
it accords men the status of persons. The implication of
that development is that the social system relies for its
very operation on the use of men not as ends but as means.

The ends are impersonal and trans-human. In consequence, personal styles no longer affect social structure. Modern religious movements no longer have real significance for the social system, although they may offer individual salvation—at times, explicitly salvation from the system. The cults reject the instrumental rationality of modern society and the large-scale impersonal social order. They pronounce their distrust of the scientific, routinized, and bureaucratic procedures on which modern social systems depend, and demand a rediscovery of the self by avenues of exploration previously forbidden. But whereas earlier religious revivals, revivalism within a religious tradition, led to a reintegration of the individual within the social order, the new cults propose to take the individual out of his society, and to save him by the wisdom of some other, wholly exotic body of belief and practice.

So it is that a curious balance of religious trade occurs in the world today. The Christian Churches, and in particular the dissenting sects, still send out missionaries to developing countries to disseminate teachings that militate against magic, witchcraft, and the vibrant and manifold religiosity of those countries, and which thus contribute to an incipient process of secularization. Meanwhile, the West imports the gurus, mantras, magic, and Messiahs from many of the same places. The justification that the early hippies found for the use of drugs in the Peyote cult of the North American Indians; the offer of a Korean Messiah to complete the principles of Christianity; and the conscious decision of the leader of the Hare Krishna cult to establish a following in the United States—are all different examples of the new patterns of cultural importation. Little attention is paid to the social effects in their societies of origin of these religious styles: they are imported and imitated essentially because they offer something to the individual, to save him from his own society. While some men in the Third World now seek to save themselves through sects informed by what might loosely be called the Protestant ethic, some of the young people of the West seek their salvation by freeing themselves from it. This, then, is not so much a revival of religion in its cultural significance as its rejection, together with the rejection of the society in which it was nourished.

The sources of secularization and the appeal of the new cults are themselves to be found in the contemporary social situation. These phenomena are related to other aspects of social change. Secularization is intimately related to the decline of community, to increased social mobility, and to the impersonality of role-relationships. The new cults and the eclecticism that is indebted to them stand in direct continuity with the protest against all these developments which is misleadingly called 'the counter-culture'. That protest exists in many forms. Its milder versions are represented by the widely diffused life-styles of the young, including unkempt, hirsute appearance and the affectation of patched-up clothes. In extreme forms, it may be seen as student protest, football hooliganism, or even guerrilla warfare. All these things are, together with contemporary music, rock festivals, permissive life-styles, truancy, vandalism, and drugs, thrusts against social order and received cultural values.

Behind all these diverse phenomena are the demands for authentic experience, for immediacy, spontaneity, and instantaneity. However inarticulate, or even unperceived, may be the real significance of these patterns of behaviour, they represent anti-formalism, anti-structuralism, and the refusal to accept inner constraint, and an effort to destroy external constraining agencies. Modern society has become increasingly programmed, from the offerings of the media to the procedures of social selection and work activity, but the programming lacks adequate legitimation. Contemporary society is less legitimated than any previously existing social system, and part of that lack of legitimation stems from the collapse of a shared conception of transcendent order.

The traditional orientation of society and of religion was the afterlife, but there is a basic incongruity between consumer society and afterlife concerns. Producer societies are consonant with ideologies of post-mortem benefits, but consumer society demands gratification now. Need we be surprised that the Happy–Healthy–Holy organization of the Yogi Bhajan tells his thirty thousand American followers, in words that echo those of many contemporary cults and Human Potential groups, that the goal is to be 'liberated while still on earth'? Consumer society demands the rejection of the 'culture of postponement', and in its place it offers a cult of present realization. Human suffering, and even human waiting, are rejected, together with those elaborate roundabout procedures of capital formation and production that have been essential for the development of the advanced industrial society.

Instead, there must be immediate access to direct experience, for which neither socialization nor learning are really necessary. Even those of the new cults that do inculcate a rigorous discipline also emphasize that there are immediate benefits for converts, 'gains' as the Scientologists call them. It is wholly characteristic for new religious movements to facilitate mobility, quicker ways to the spiritual top, that cut through the encrustations of ritual, institutionalism, intellectualism, and the whole apparatus of scholarship that religions tend to accrete. Thus the instancy and the urgency are not in themselves new, but their combination with intense subjectivism, rejection of the culture, and the preoccupation with the self is new.

The new cults do not serve society. They are indeed almost irrelevant to it, since their sources of inspiration are exotic, esoteric, subjective, and subterranean. Truth comes from far places, or from lower social strata, or from hitherto untapped depths of the self or the psyche. Thus, conceptions of socially inspired self-restraint, and co-ordination of individuals within the wider society, on which all on-going social systems depend, are entirely alien. Instead of restraint there is an emphasis on pleasure. (Some cults do, as we have seen, impose severe discipline on their adherents, but this is the discipline of virtuosi. It is not the sustained restraint useful in the everyday world, but rather the discipline which, paradoxically, in itself becomes almost a self-indulgence.) Institutionalized religions gradually replaced local magic with a universal ethic, but the new cults ignore the wider ethical prescriptions on which alone a sustained culture can rest, and sometimes specifically endorse local, personal, or community special pleading for dispensations from the normal forces of causation: such pleading itself sometimes amounts to belief, implicit and sometimes even explicit, in the miraculous, and even the magical. Instead of being agencies of general socialization, some of these movements reject precisely the cultivated aspirations and pretences on which culture depends. They seek mystification rather than rationalization. The exotic is a good in its own right to which concession must be made, rather than the exotic being modified and reconciled to a resilient native tradition.

H

When the new cults do employ some measure of discipline, as in their ascetic exercises some of them do, it is
clear that their discipline is for the commune and not for
the world. Their verbal slanging-matches, mutual criticism,
hazing, ordeals, punishments, and retributions (in groups
such as Synanon and Scientology) are means of dissipating
communal tensions and reinforcing solidarity. But these
are rediscoveries of ancient techniques, and they are not
socially transformative. They are ascetic exercises that are
relevant only within the cult commune, not a recovery of
those patterns of well-diffused asceticism with which particular social strata built up the economic and social order
of the West.

What the modern world has lost in losing its traditional
culture has been the basis for legitimated control. That
loss has occurred as our social order has shifted its basic
locus of operation from local community to a societal
system, a nation-wide coherently integrated structure of
roles and institutions. In this circumstance control ceases
to be local and human, and increasingly depends on technical devices, legal (rather than customary) provisions, and
bureaucratic procedures. It becomes increasingly mechan-
ized, technologized, computerized, and electronicized (the
only words we can use to describe the process frighten us
a little; so they should). This process in itself has produced
a human response of protest. Since the new agencies of
control—from planning regulations and compulsory pur-
chase to such simple things as parking arrangements—are
unsupported by a well-legitimated and sanctioned set of
inner dispositions and attitudes, and an objective code of
morality, they appear arbitrary and inhuman, and they
are abrasive in their operation. In the past, restraints were
mediated by human agents, but in our large-scale social

systems we dehumanize even the human agents of social control and socialization. We eliminate affectivity and the diffuse concern that once accompanied man's control of at least local and communal affairs. We need not be surprised if effective socialization goes by default.

In this context the new cults and the new subcultures become, simultaneously, protest at what is happening; an exaggeration and intensification of its effects; and the search for an alternative (often quite explicitly a search for a truly human encounter, by sharing emotional experience, by touching and embracing another human being, and a search for community). The cults, like the demonstrations, and even the vandalism, represent not only protest: they also express resentment and anguish. New cults often establish communes, and despite their many innovations, they clearly cater to a conservative demand for community —a demand that can no longer be expressed in the now discredited traditional terms.

Christianity was an effective religious system as long as cultural constraints were solemnized in community life. It functioned to legitimate moral and social order. But once anonymity and impersonality became the dominant experience of man in western society, so Christianity, like any institutionalized religion, lost its grip on culture. No religion can solemnize electronic controls, parking meters, and computers. They require no legitimations and depend on no process of socialization. At its best, over its long slow growth, Christianity mediated relationships of authority, helped balance social control and self-restraint, provided a moral order coloured with myth to rationalize local action in cosmic terms, and reinforced group solidarity with imposed ritual practice. It strengthened boundaries, induced restraint, reasserted principles of internal cohesion and external distinctions. Its certainty and its intolerance were concomitants of its power to maintain order, both moral and political. It decreed what was appropriate action, and who were proper persons. All this is gone, and even its faintest echo occasions protest today. But Christianity is not itself the object of that protest: it is indeed irrelevant now to the terms of the debate. The protest is against the fabric of contemporary society, and it is perhaps worth while to isolate a number of elements that provide the social context both for secularization and for counter-secularity as expressed in the new cult movements.

A little-recognized consequence of our dependence on new techniques and the speed of their change is that this process devalues human experience. Whereas experience was once a virtue in a man, it is now a handicap to him. An experienced worker is experienced only with old techniques, his skills are out-dated. Young, newly qualified men are wanted. But the old worker is also the older man, and his obsolescence as a worker is irrelevantly carried over to his quality as a human being. Several consequences ensue. Age is devalued, and youth is over-valued. Technical skills become detached from moral wisdom, even within the context of the work situation itself, and of course much more widely. The socialization of the young does not proceed except in strictly technical expertise. And the continuity of the culture is placed in jeopardy.

Modern society depends upon extensive mobility, and mobility creates anonymous publics. At one time an individual needed to build a stable reputation as a person of character and integrity. But in anonymous contexts reputation is irrelevant. All that the individual need do is to manipulate his image. The self becomes a more powerful point of reference as communal life declines in significance.

One need not be surprised that the self is a major focus of our new religions. Mobility is associated with the break-down of community and with the loss of attachment to locality. The local community was once the almost exclusive environment of man. It was the repository of custom, and custom was the cushion of social control, even until the very recent past. But in a mobile world the individual's involvements are less mediated by persons, and more by role-performers. Custom declines, and control becomes more completely external, objective, and alien. As socialized self-control declines, so the conflict between the self-indulgent individual and the needs of social order must intensify.

Beyond the local community were once relatively stable, if by no means rigid, patterns of social stratification. The changing technical basis of the social order has occasioned widespread experience of social mobility. Individuals move through statuses without acquiring the mores, norms, or cultural dispositions that once were integrated with them. The behavioural models have gone, and with them standards of sensitivity, social responsibility, and the agencies of cultural transmission from one generation to another.[12] The very satisfactions of status, which were once based on cultural distinctions, have been reduced to crude money terms, in conformity with the instrumentalism of the contemporary social system. The widened opportunities for status enhancement have been accompanied only by increased status insecurity and by the elimination of the social sources of status gratification. The loss of notional exemplars (who, even if not always as good as they were supposed to be, none the less fulfilled an important

[12] For a fuller discussion see Bryan R. Wilson, *The Youth Culture and the Universities*, London: Faber, 1970, pp. 204-17.

function) may have significant consequences for a society in reducing the moral criteria for behaviour to expediency and opportunism.

These social processes have been accompanied by a massive redistribution of income—to the young. The young are the affluent *un*committed section of society. Since they are no longer socialized to stable expectations, they fall quickly prey to commercial exploiters, and the cycle of stimulated demand and its supply leads to the less cultivated appetite becoming the arbiter of public taste. Equivocally in many cases, but with more vigour in the new religious movements, some sections of the contemporary youth culture have already made evident their disenchantment with the commercial values of modern society. But, since even their own perceptions of culture and society are so dominantly informed by the mass media, any widespread protest is inevitably compromised.

The communications explosion of our times has itself contributed powerfully to the process of secularization by the diffusion of widely diverse and relatively disordered knowledge. Just what people should know, and in what order they should acquire knowledge, is something that our contemporary society has lost the power to assert. Modern man lives in a random supermarket of knowledge that is in fact a maze. Whereas once he learned slowly things that he needed to know for his work, for his life in a given locality, for his comportment of himself among others, now knowledge loses its structure and its social significance in many areas of everyday life. The consequences are numerous. Personal growth is challenged and perhaps stultified by over-exposure to an abundance of expertism. A plurality of styles is offered that leads to facile cultural relativism which destroys the individual's confidence in his own culture and which leaves unmanned the cultural defences of any given society. Even the institutionalized systems of knowledge and procedures for learning, as embodied in universities, are assaulted and undermined. In such disorder, and with such powerful agencies at work, is it surprising that some should come to believe that the only authentic knowledge comes from societies the cultures of which are not yet much affected by the mass media?

In western society the mass media have been principal agencies in the dissemination of modern hedonism and entertainment values. Consumer societies need an ethic of hedonism, of course, but the ethic has been diffused through the entertainment industry, which, in the course of a few short decades, has become an all-pervasive presence in the life of modern man. From the opportunity for organized entertainment for perhaps two or three hours a week, men have, in the span of no more than forty years, come to expect entertainment throughout a greater part of their waking lives, as an accompaniment to work, as a significant goal in education, as an inexhaustible supply in the growing proportion of leisure time available in advanced industrial societies. That this process has led to the paradox of routinized pleasure and to boredom is perhaps not surprising. The new cults, too, are equivocal. They offer men ways to get more out of living, and they emphasize complete happiness, even if they also canvass their own ascetic practices as the only way in which such happiness may be attained.

Finally, one feature of the consumer society may not be ignored, and that is the dependence of these societies on maintaining a balance of supply and demand, however much demand may be manipulated. Consumer society is a society where men learn to sell, and as salesmen often learn their trade, to sell first of all themselves. When men have to sell themselves, to assume dispositions that they do not genuinely feel, in the interests of narrow instrumental ends, a process of widespread human prostitution then occurs. New levels of distrust are reached, as men acquire the art of cynicism that is necessary for their very survival. In the face of modern advertising, everyone must be a cynic: to believe is to run the serious risk of being betrayed. Cynicism learned as an art of survival is unlikely to remain confined to commercial relationships or to an appraisal of the mass media. It becomes a permanent posture in the face of all authorities and all belief systems.

If these features are the occasion of our contemporary discontents, it is also clear that those most affected by them are likely to be the young, yet they are also that section of the population that has the energy, the enthusiasm, and the idealism to suppose that there must be an alternative to the present social system. Since they are least committed socially, it is not surprising that they constitute the greater part of the clientele of the new movements. The movements offer salvation not by recourse to intellectual systems, but to experiences that enhance the emotions and reduce inhibitions. As traditional procedures of socialization break down, it is not surprising that the search into the self should appeal to young people. Recourse to the self and its emotions is supported by appeal to the exotic, to arcane, hitherto unknown and uncompromised sources of wisdom from societies innocent of western corruptions. The attraction of ancient wisdom or primitive cultures may be further reinforced by the authority of the charismatic leader, and charisma is more readily accepted when coming from an unfamiliar source. All of this is subsumed in a religious system: no other body of knowledge would suffice. Religious knowledge and practice is arbitrary, transcending all empirico-rational tests as irrelevant, and providing overarching meaning and final legitimations to those who commit themselves totally, who in giving all will receive all.

Such is the complete alternative for those disenchanted with the modern world. It offers, as nothing else can, world transcendence *and* immediate benefits, and each movement claims to provide involvement in a vigorous local community and affiliation to a world-wide organization. That religious commitment leads to curious paradoxes should not surprise us. Insisting on self-realization, some movements impose severe disciplines on adherents—the very discipline which so many young people in affluent, permissive society have been denied. (Cultures of poverty demand discipline: affluent cultures make the disciplined man seem archaic, but when ex-hippies join some new cults they may, having rejected the 'uptight' quality of contemporary society, spend considerable time learning what in effect is being 'uptight' again, albeit according to a different set of rules.) Nor need it be surprising that, in a predominantly secular society in which most activities are conducted without reference to the supernatural, young men and women go on what would once have been called 'spiritual pilgrimages', though they are sometimes closer in style to what contemporaries regard as 'trips'. In the cultic milieu of large urban centres, such trips may be a recurrent experience for some who drift from one movement to another.

The new cults are sometimes claimed as the advance guard of the 'counter-culture', and in some measure, and despite the diversity of their content, this idea is part of the ideology to which they themselves subscribe. But will they really produce a new culture, in the sense of a sustained set of values and life-patterns, with appropriate symbolic expression, that facilitate a high measure of social and institutional integration for modern society? Nothing about the new cults, or about the general character of existing social currents, suggests that they will. They are not so much the progenitors of a counter-culture, as random anti-cultural assertions. What is called the 'counter-culture' is indeed little more than a range of phenomena from the hippies, flower people, speed freaks, Jesus people, Hare Krishna devotees, and the rest, who do not represent a culture at all, but just a congeries of options in a plural society—a diverse set of options 'out'.

There is indeed even serious reason to doubt the capacity of many cults to sustain themselves over the long period in any case. To persist they must become institutionalized, yet their primary appeal is in their informal, loose spontaneity. Exotic novelty provides them with their initial attractiveness, but once the exotic is known its appeal must wane. The cults have in the main already set themselves over against the wider society, so losing the opportunity to influence it directly. They are preoccupied with young adults, and in general have no techniques for the socialization of the children of members. Hitherto, religious movements have persisted primarily by socializing and eventually incorporating the descendants of their initial converts. Finally, the very process of social change in which they have emerged continues. In so far as they are conditioned by the time of their emergence, they must undergo adaptation in order to persist: as yet few of the cults show a capacity for adaptation.

Some of the new movements, and this is most applicable to those that embody explicit protest against contemporary society, have succeeded by resorting to the methods of the capitalist society to which they object. Just as the popular entertainers who made their fortunes by singing protest songs had to be produced, publicized, packaged, and marketed, so it was with the new religious movements. Like Bob Dylan and the Rolling Stones, new therapeutic systems and new transcendental philosophies succeed in the world as commercial commodities, promoted for profit within the capitalist business system. Even if the more respectable religious movements use the earnings they make solely for further propaganda, and this may often be the case, none the less, they depend on contemporary capitalist methods of sales promotion. Eventually there are disenchanted former converts who discover all too sadly how even the most idealistic and wholly-other religious metaphysic may in day-to-day affairs be compromised by the methods it adopts to disseminate its message.

Whatever means they employ to disseminate their philosophies, some of the new cults do attempt to create a distinct and even ascetic alternative way of life for their devotees. But even this is not the basis from which a new culture can be created. These are virtuoso religions, prescribing asceticism appropriate and sustainable only within the closed community. It cannot be transferred to wider publics: it is a regimen suited to the commune, and particularly to the commune that is not itself self-sufficient but which depends on remittances, resources, and recruits from the wider society. The ascetic does not provide an ethical basis for the life of men in a large-scale societal system.

In their diverse ways of deviating from the dominant society, the cults offer another way of life for the self-selected few rather than an alternative culture for mankind. The fact that they are recruited in very large part from the young is an intimation of their lack of durability. If their appeal is essentially to the young, then they must be reminded that 'youth's a stuff will not endure'. In so far as their appeal will be affected by wider currents of social change, tomorrow's youth may make its generational protest in different terms. It is perhaps because the cults can be so readily assimilated to the youth culture that they have been identified as an alternative culture. If, as we have suggested, they do not represent a serious and viable alternative to traditional culture in the West, their emergence should at least indicate to us the nature of the widespread breakdown of our culture, and the fact that that breakdown arises in considerable part in the context of generational protest. That protest arises for reasons, some of which we have explored, and is directed against the rational and technical developments that I have also indicated as major contributors to the secularization process. Secularization, I have suggested, is the major contemporary transformation of religion, against which the cults are likely to be no more than transient and volatile gestures of defiance.

The erosion of the traditional culture of western society has been in process, unevenly and spasmodically, for a considerable time. We have been learning or half-learning how to live without a culture, or with the rags and tatters of an earlier culture still clutched about the parts of us that we least care to expose. Capitalism has itself been an agency in this process. As capitalism became culturally neutral, indifferent to human values, and willing to make a profit from any cultural or anti-cultural commodities, so the viability of traditional values declined. *Laissez-faire* economics inevitably led to *laissez-faire* morality, and the underpinnings of culture—a socially diffused and shared moral sense—are thus eroded. Modern societies have ceased to depend upon an integrated consensus of values as the basis of their cohesion. Society, as distinct from the agglomeration of communities that in the past made up the larger entity loosely referred to as 'society', is a coherent, large-scale integrated system, held together by techniques and procedures not by values. Culture, in advanced societies, ceases to be integrative: it becomes a super-numerary item, as society shifts from being a moral to being a technical system. Permissiveness and pluralism in-dicate the social insignificance and the systemic insulation of culture—and of religion, which was the chief carrier of the cultural inheritance. Outside their role-performances, men are in a sense liberated. Their personal beliefs, life-styles, choices in the use of leisure time, cease to be of much consequence in advanced societies, at least in the short run.

In the long run, however, belief and commitment may matter, both for the continuance of social order and the well-being of individuals. But even those of the new move-ments that do mobilize commitment and do demand discipline are not organized to disseminate an effective ethic for a whole society. Many of these movements openly reject discipline and ignore, where they do not impugn, a social ethic. In doing so they make manifest their anti-cultural orientation. All cultures control liberty, but the new cults preach liberation, and sometimes libertarianism. The modern credo of 'Doing your own thing' is implicit where it is not explicit in their conception of how life should be lived. Professor Robert A. Evans, a modern theologian, quotes with approval one of the gurus of the so-called counter-culture, Frederick Perls, who expresses his thoughts thus:

> I do my thing, and you do your thing.
> I am not in this world to live up to your
>   expectations
> And you are not in this world to live up
>   to mine.
> You are you and I am I.
> And if by chance we find each other—
>   —It's beautiful.[13]

No persisting society can leave people to do their own thing. No culture can flourish unless men share expectations about each other and their behaviour. No amount of sensitivity training can substitute for the sustained concern for the cultivation of truly human talents and capacities, which is a work that takes at least a childhood, and perhaps a lifetime. Civilization, as the business of dealing with our fellow men with care and courtesy, and of discovering the principles by which to order our lives, depends on learning to 'live up to' the higher conceptions that others have of us. We need our pretences, and sometimes we succeed in turning them into our realities. As for what it is like 'when we find each other', it may be beautiful, but generally in the modern world it is routine. Most meetings are, and must be, structured—but if we can, by shared moral training, by careful cultivation, make the routine into the human, we achieve more than what is promised by the spasmodic experience of getting 'high' or 'switched on', as if ecstasy were the only mode in which joy might be attained.

[13] Cited in Robert A. Evans, *Belief and the Counter Culture*, Philadelphia: The Westminster Press, 1971, p. 50.

Professor Evans describes the 'counter-culture', of which he approves, as giving priority to 'experience, creativity, symbolic communication, and openness to the transcendent that brings about a transformation of consciousness'.[14] These things can never be the priorities of any social system. At most they can be priorities for élites, or for parasites on a wider social order, most of whose members will have to live by learning and intellect (their own or that of others), by routine and imitation, by increasingly rational means of communication, and by at best occasional behest to the transcendental. In limited measure, and it may be a measure that some would wish to enlarge, all of these things persist in on-going cultures, for some inevitably more than for others, but they are not the central items of life anywhere except in small, privileged, and ultimately inconsequential communities. If a transformation of the individual's consciousness is achieved, it must not be supposed that this, in contexts such as these, will lead to a transformation of the social order, upon which the consciousness of the mass of mankind will always depend.

It may well be that an integrated culture is now a thing of the past in the West (and perhaps throughout the world). Modern societies rest on different bases of control. And that perhaps is the cause of our contemporary discontents. We know no moral order to give meaning to our social order. We have lost faith in the vision of a cumulative and progressive culture which cherished the products of the human spirit, elevated man's humanity, guarded the inheritance of past societies, and rejoiced in the widening prospect of the richer inheritance of posterity. The process by which all this has come about is intimately associated

[14] Ibid., p. 23.

with the process of secularization, the dominant transformation of religion in our time.

Yet, if this is so, this fact alone should not lead us into
a facile espousal of the self-styled 'counter-culture'. Its
priorities, as Professor Evans lists them, are, of course,
the priorities of the cults. They are elements, some of
which, although never central, and although almost all
lost in the rationalized society of the West, had their place
in our culture in the past. That place was, however, a
delimited place in which these elements were controlled:
experience was disciplined by intellect; creativity was
restrained by well-tried routines and widely accepted
rules; symbolic communication was progressively circumscribed by the need for empirical precision; communality
was superseded by societal organization; and openness to
the transcendent was set at life's margins (birth, death, and
Sundays) as men relied increasingly on the pragmatic. The
friability of the new cults lies in their attempt to recover in
some pristine and unattenuated form these aspects of a
culture, without regard to the necessity of institutionaliza-
tion and social control which religion must make as it
adapts from its communal location to the needs of men in
an integrated societal system. The compromise inevitably
leads to the loss of religious vitality, but that is part of the
evolutionary process: religions are always dying. In the
modern world it is not clear that they have any prospect
of rebirth.